THE ALTERNATE
SURVIVOR

6/26/06

Sarah
Always Rock on!

Love,
Sue

THE ALTERNATE SURVIVOR

BY

SUE POLLARD

With

MATTHEW BERG

Woodfall Press

http://www.woodfallpress.com

Published by
Woodfall Press
P.O. Box #141
Medway, MA 02053

ISBN 0-9785791-0-0

Printed in the United States of America

~ Sue's Dedication ~

For my Husband Bob
And my Three Beautiful Children
Miranda, Lauren, Justin
For Always Supporting and Believing in Me!

And to My Dear Friend, Jesus Christ,
For giving me the Gift of Perseverance!

~ Matt's Dedication ~

To My Parents:
My Mother, for her unwavering support and
encouragement
My Father, for the example he set by working hard
and making his own way

Table of Contents

Prologue

How it all began

I came so close. Like many of you, I racked my brain to come up with a clever and interesting audition video. I tried to give fun and challenging answers to the questions that were asked on the application. I hoped they might be able to see and hear the real me coming through in the words I wrote and on the video. Because I knew that if I were selected to be a participant on *Survivor 6: Amazon* that I could *win*. And if it were possible for a person to will a thing to happen, I tried that, too.

Against the best hopes of even my own stubborn sense of pride I found myself getting shots for malaria and other tropical diseases only days before the shooting was scheduled to begin. I was the first alternate and one of the women finalists had broken her toe. I was only days away from becoming a participant on *Survivor* 6. My adventure in the Amazon was about to begin!

But then, heartbreakingly, it all fell apart. The woman (Shawna, for the fans out there) decided to go despite her broken toe. And she was cleared by the show.

I was devastated. The *Survivor* casting process had been a long and emotionally challenging road for me. I'd experienced everything from excitement to despair to joy to frustration and ultimately to elation. In the end, there was a gnawing sense of bitterness and of having been robbed. But I'm getting a bit ahead of myself. So why don't I start this thing over from the beginning?

My name is Sue Pollard. I'm a happily married wife of 25 years, a mother of three beautiful children, Chair of the local School Board, and a three-time entrepreneur in my home state of Maine.

The Alternate Survivor

Those who truly know me understand at least two things about me: The first is that I have a boundless supply of energy, and the second is that I don't quit. Both of these facts will come into play quite a bit in my story so it's important to remember them!

To give you an idea what I mean: If I go out to sell ten accounts for my business and I only sell eight, I won't quit until I get those last two. They gnaw at me. They keep me awake at night. I can't stop thinking about them.

And it was just this aspect of my personality that, before I even knew what *Survivor* was all about, had convinced my friend that I would be a great contestant. Here's how it happened:

I was working at my restaurant in Ogunquit, Maine. At the time I was waking up early and I would be on the job each day by 7:00 A.M. and would often find myself cleaning up at night until 10:00 or even 11:00 P.M. I rarely took a moment to pause and catch my breath.

But on this day, a very dear friend of mine named Richard Payeur was in for lunch. Richard was a regular and someone who could actually coax me into sitting down and joining him for a moment or two every now and again.

We were, and still are, such great friends and I admire him because he is such a hard worker. He is a building contractor in town and very well liked and respected.

Well on this one day he took me aside and asked me if I ever watched *Survivor*. I told him that I wasn't really a sit-down television watcher—that I was usually too busy. (As he knew, I was always going 100 miles per hour!) But Richard watched the show faithfully and he told me that if there were anyone he knew who could not only make it on *Survivor*, but *win* it, he thought that it was me.

I said, "Come on, Richard!" But he was persistent.

"If I were to go home and print you out an application would you fill it out and do a video and send it in?"

I shrugged my shoulders. "Sure. Why not?"

But while it was only a whim at first I became more and more captivated by the idea of being on *Survivor*. Since I was a little girl I'd wanted to be on TV. I was always, and still am, so outgoing and competitive and got such a thrill out of entertaining people. I just really enjoyed the spotlight.

How great would it be to be on *Survivor*? Not only would I be on TV but I'd be doing something outrageous: challenging other competitive people for a huge prize of a million dollars! I must admit I relished the thought of the contests and the attention. And once I had this all in my mind I just couldn't stop thinking about it and I wanted to make it.

And, of course, once I start thinking about doing something not only do I have to finish it but I have to win it! My family aside, you might say I came to want it more than anything in my life.

Pollard & Berg

One

Applying for Survivor

Whenever I talk about my story I'm always surprised at how many other people out there either sent in an application video of their own or are very close to someone who did. The six degrees of separation effect seems more like two or three when it comes to *Survivor* applicants! It's reassuring to me that so many people out there are just as crazy as I am!

Almost universally, everyone remembers the video-making process as one that was full of fun and laughter when shooting, full of pain and frustration to edit and prepare, and an exercise in anxiety to submit. To me it was almost like having a personal investment in a lottery ticket!

But as fun as it was, the first part (shooting the video) wasn't exactly easy either. How could I tell the casting crew at *Survivor* that I was the right person for the show in only 3 minutes?

My first couple of attempts were pretty silly. For the first attempt I had my daughters Miranda and Lauren tape me as if I were eating worms and dirt. Of course once we watched it on TV it looked a lot more like crushed Oreo cookies and dark brown gummy worms (which is exactly what it was) than I'd hoped. On my second attempt, I had Miranda tape me diving off our house into our swimming pool. It was a somewhat scary stunt in that my pool is several feet away from the roof-line of my house, but on video it just didn't have the same effect as it did in person. And I could only imagine how many videos *Survivor* may have received of people doing far more spectacular things.

But the more I thought about it after watching the footage from these two videos the more I realized how silly I was being. And I decided that I was going to do a tape that would show the people at *Survivor* what I was really like.

We started again after Miranda and I fought about who was going to eat the rest of the Oreos and gummy worms. Ha! But seriously, I put some real thought into my next video. I really wanted this video to show everyone who watched it who Sue Pollard *is*: outgoing, with a little bit of a wild side, and lots of charisma.

So the next day my daughters helped out by videotaping me again. I picked out the perfect outfit—I had on my shortest shorts with my great legs (if I do say so myself!), my high leather boots and my short jean jacket. I borrowed my friend Darin's motorcycle. I had the motor revving and I looked into the camera as my 12 year old daughter Lauren was videotaping and I said "Are you looking for a girl with high energy, highly competitive, driven to beat the band and a little sexy too? Someone who is going to make you want to watch

that show every week? Then you've found your girl!"
Then I drive off just as smooth as can be. Sweeeet!

The next clip shows me standing on the side
of my jeep wrangler with the top down in the full
wetsuit that I wear for surfing. I was acting like I
was getting ready to go surfing. My words into the
camera as Lauren was videoing were:

"I'm 44 years old. I think I'm in pretty darn
good shape. I've had three children—the first one
weighing 10 lbs, 3 oz. Obviously surviving will come
pretty easy to me!

"I love being competitive. I love people. And
I just enjoy life.

"I would consider myself, if I were selected,
the Lucille Ball of *Survivor*. When they talk about
bringing one luxury item, well there would be only
one luxury item I would bring and of course that
would be my red lipstick."

I put on my lipstick and smiled.

"No one has ever seen me without me having
my red lipstick on. And at this point I'm going to
leave you with a clip I did being Chair of the School
Board—my closing remarks at graduation last week,
actually".

Then I winked at the camera, drove off in my jeep with my surfboard in the back and my license plate clearly showing "SUZIPOO".

Okay, that went great! I was excited! And I thought that the clip I had selected for the end of my three-minute video was even better—since it showed what I'm like in "real life" (when I'm not trying get onto television).

The last segment starts by showing the Principal of Wells High School, Becky Brink, introducing me by saying, "Sue Pollard, our School Committee Chair, would like to say a few words."

Up until this point in the ceremony there had been a few speeches given that seemed like they took hours—you know the kind. So I walked up to the mike and said, "I promise it will be short!" The crowd clapped and I just about got a standing ovation that seemed to last for five minutes.

With a big smile I marched up to the podium with my high heels clacking on the wooden floor of the auditorium.

"I first want to say that I am proud to stand up here as a school committee chair person and tell each one of you how very proud we are of all of you.

Class of 2002, you have been very impressive throughout the years. I have known a lot of you since kindergarten and you have grown up to be outstanding adults."

There was some brief applause before I continued.

"I was riding around in the car the other day and I was thinking to myself, '*What am going to say to you guys?*' and the song, *The World's Greatest,* came on. I thought to myself that the next time someone asks you who you are, you should stand up tall, look them in the face and say, *'I'm the World's Greatest because I did it!'*"

Now the whole audience clapped, whistled, and screamed 'You go, girl!'. I smiled and held my head up high with pride.

"Graduating from high school is one of the first big steps you can take in your life. It's the first big step in your future and being out there on your own.

"If I can give you a little advice I would say: *keep family a priority.* Family is one of the most important parts of your life. And it's obvious (as I put my arms out) that they love you very much and you wouldn't be here without them!

"You're going to go out tonight to party and celebrate. And tomorrow, when you get up in that great big world, whatever career you decide to do—whether it's a CEO of a company or sweeping floors—you give it your best everyday. And I guarantee that where you're sweeping floors you will be the CEO of that company!

"I would also like to say to be good to people and treat people the way you want to be treated. And remember: have fun with whatever you do because enthusiasm is contagious!"

At that point I stopped and looked at the class of 2002 and said with a great big smile: "AND ALWAYS, ALWAYS ROCK ON!" I held my hands high, each with pinkie and index finger extended in the *rock on* sign.

The entire class stood and smiled, clapped and cheered. "YES, Mrs. Pollard!" And a few smart-alecks even shouted "Go Suzipoo!" (in reference to the name of my business).

I sat back down with the Superintendent as a crowd of people continued to clap and whistle. And that was the end of my three-minute video.

I can remember I wanted this video to be perfect. I had clips from so many different things and I had to narrow it down to three minutes. So I took it to a good friend of mine and we literally worked on it for at least five hours, cutting here and there and fading the clips in and out. Making sure that it was perfect, I even made a label for the VHS tape that had a great picture of me on the front and under the picture it read:

CBS Meet Sue Pollard, Your Next Survivor

I really thought the tape had come out great and I was very proud of it—even though a three-minute tape had taken me almost a week to complete! I showed it to my husband and my daughters and they loved it. I remember hugging my girls and telling them what a great job they had done filming me because I am sure that they must have been frustrated with me by the time we were done. I can't tell you how many times I would say one of the words wrong when we were taping, and then say "Oh, Ca-ca!", and they would both laugh. I remember Miranda saying at one point, "Mom, maybe we should send a blooper tape with this too!" (Probably wouldn't have been a bad idea!) And we would laugh again.

We kept doing take after take, laughing a little less each time maybe—as the novelty wore off and we just wanted to be done—but we were still having fun up until the very end. When we were done with the taping I think my girls could recite the script we'd written word for word. Trust me, we were becoming professionals!

To this day we still joke about it and sometimes, out of the blue, they will recite something I said on the tape because they know it will get a laugh out of me. We didn't keep an exact count, but jokingly said "Take two!" at least twenty times. It was a bit exhausting frankly, but it was fun. And now looking back on it, it was also a wonderful bonding experience with my daughters. We'd overcome a trial of endurance together and kept our good humor throughout. I'm sure we'll talk about making that video for the rest of our lives!

I know that many of you reading this book can probably relate to making your own three-minute video and how you probably changed it twenty times. I mean, lets face it, you don't know what they're looking for, right? But after playing around with a couple of silly "gag" shots I realized that a gag or a stunt wasn't going to sell me to the casting crew. So I decided to send in a video of just who I am. And it sure seems to have worked for me—since I ultimately would make it as far as first alternate for the women of *Survivor: Amazon*!

I really felt good sending in the application and the VHS tape. I can remember making sure everything was perfect. I double-checked to be sure that the label was in the correct place, and probably checked the address itself ten times to make sure that everything was right:

> *Survivor*
> *2801 Ocean Park Blvd.*
> *Santa Monica, California 90405*

I was meticulous. And I even overnighted the package to make sure it got there in plenty of time.

I can remember anxiously getting on my computer the next day to check on the tracking number and *bingo!* It was received in Santa Monica at 3:07 P.M! At that point I knew that I'd done everything that I could and that it would just be a waiting game. I tried to put the whole thing behind me, and to accept that I was no longer in control of the process. It was like I'd thrown a switch inside my head. I let go of my excitement. I let go of the anxious tension that had built up in me while I was filling out the application and making the video. Honestly, I really didn't think I would ever hear back. And only a very small part of me thought I even had a chance.

About a week had passed, and I was in my office above the restaurant doing paperwork when the phone rang.

"Hello."

"Hello, is Sue Pollard there?"

"This is she."

"This is Martha from *Survivor*."

Well I just was floored. I managed an upbeat, "Hi!"

"We got your application and your video and we think you would be a great candidate for *Survivor*."

"That's awesome!" I was so excited. All of a sudden I started thinking about how cool it would be to be on *Survivor*! But Martha kept bringing me back to earth.

"First off, you can't tell anyone about this besides your husband. I mean you can't tell anyone."

No biggie, I thought—even though it wouldn't be easy. But what choice did I have? I said, "O.K."

Then Martha said she needed to meet with me and would be in Boston on August eighth and ninth. I told her I could make it on the eighth.

"Sounds great," she said. She would send me all the information and directions. She said she looked forward to meeting me and I told her I couldn't wait. So I hung up the phone and sat back in my chair, letting it all sink in. This thing was really happening!

The Alternate Survivor

If I had thrown a switch in my head to shut off my emotions earlier, when I thought I'd never hear back about my application, well it was like someone had stuck my finger in an electrical socket when I got off the phone with Martha after that first call.

Emotions like I have never felt coursed through me. I'm normally a high-energy person, but I'd never felt so much excitement in all of my life. I remember hanging the phone up from that phone call like it was yesterday. I was riding an incredible, surging, natural high. My whole body felt charged with energy. I could almost feel the blood pumping through my veins. And I think that if someone had told me that I needed to swim across the Atlantic to claim my prize I'd have jumped right in. It was a powerful and incredible sensation that I can only imagine no drug could ever touch.

Still off-balance from the phone call I stood up, gathered myself for a moment, and then couldn't help myself but to race down the stairs of my restaurant. It was going to be hard to go back to work and act normal. I was literally being overcome with excitement but I couldn't tell anyone!

I remember that one of my employees, a girl named Peggy—who I adore, said, "What are you so happy about?"

I looked at her and smiled with a big sigh. "I'm just having a great day, Peggy!"

Minutes later I hopped into my Jeep Wrangler with the top down and started driving down one of the back roads I love to ride on. I put on the song I had mentioned in my graduation speech, R. Kelly's "The Worlds Greatest," and cranked it up. It was a beautiful summer day that I'd have been enjoying anyway for the day's sake and for the wind in my hair. But the high I was riding from the news about *Survivor* hadn't lessened at all, so I was on top of the world. I don't think I've ever enjoyed a ride in my Jeep more than I enjoyed that one.

I walked into my house to find both my daughters in the kitchen. I burst into the room and they looked at me like I was crazy (nothing unusual there, of course!). Then I blurted it out, "They called! *Survivor* called!" And then they went crazy too!

All three of us were jumping up and down like we were teenagers (which was actually the case for 2 out of 3 of us, anyway!). Miranda said, "Let's go find Dad!" and so off we went. My husband runs his own landscaping business and was out on the road at one of his client's homes. We drove around and couldn't find him for about a half an hour.

When we finally found him, the same song was still blaring out of the open Jeep. Of course that didn't surprise my husband at all. It was very normal for the girls and I to pull up with music blaring! I jumped out of the car and ran over to him.

"Bob, they called! *Survivor* called!"

He smiled, hugged me and said, "So what does that mean?"

I answered him with confidence, "Well I'm taking it as the obvious first step to making it onto *Survivor*! And that's the only step I need!"

He hugged me again. "That's great, Honey! So what's next?"

"Well, I guess I'd better get ready."

"Well, we're all with you. So let's help you get into the best shape of your life!"

That night we started training very hard. We climbed a mountain ten miles from my house called Mount Agamenticus. We would end up having a lot of fun climbing that mountain over the next two weeks. Every night, and I mean *every* night, my daughter Miranda would drive the whole family to the bottom of the mountain—including our new puppy at the time: Teddy, an Old English sheepdog. Miranda just got her permit so she loved to drive any chance she got.

We would leave for the mountain around 6:30 P.M. when my husband got home from work. Miranda, Lauren, Justin, Bob, Teddy and I would all pile into the Expedition and off we'd go.

When we'd get to the mountain Bob, Justin, Teddy and I would start by walking and jogging up the *three-mile hill from Hell*, as we affectionately called it! By the second week we were running up that hill and taking side trails as though we were in the jungle. It was hard, but fun! I was committed to this and my family was right by my side all the way.

The Alternate Survivor

I trained hard for the show—beyond just hiking up and down Mount Agamenticus, too. I would get up mornings and ride my bike, rain or shine, for five miles every day. I was lifting weights. And I swam every day, too! I was ready for *Survivor* and I was taking it very seriously. I remember being in such a focused state of mind. No physical weakness was going to keep me from winning any of the challenges. I was determined that when, not if, I was ultimately selected to be on *Survivor*: Amazon, that I was going to give it everything I had.

###

The day Martha called I had wanted to tell the world and been told that I couldn't. But besides my family, I had to tell Richard Payeur because I would not have even tried out for *Survivor* if it wasn't for him. I remember it well. I found out in the afternoon and after telling just my husband, Lauren and Miranda, I decided that I had to tell Richard, too. I drove everywhere looking for him but he was nowhere to be found.

Eventually I remembered that I did have a restaurant to run and had to get back to work. So the next day during lunch I was in the kitchen and I told the girls out front to come and get me if Richard Payeur came in.

It was about 12:45 in the afternoon and one of the girls came back into the kitchen to let me know that he was there.

I was wearing a smile that a crowbar couldn't have taken off my face when he noticed me approaching. He looked at me somewhat strangely. He was used to my being happy and upbeat but I think he could tell that something was making me even happier than I normally was. He smirked good-naturedly, "What are you smiling about?"

"Come here for a minute." I gestured for him to come up to my office. He seemed somewhat surprised but followed me anyway.

Once we were inside my office and the door was closed, I almost exploded, "Richard, *Survivor* called and I made the first cut!"

"You're kidding me! It's not that I'm surprised but you've got to be kidding me!"

"No, I'm not, Richard!"

He gave me a giant hug and said, "Wow, I *knew* you could make it!"

We were both acting like I was leaving the next day and had already made it onto *Survivor*. Just like me, he had a huge grin on his face and couldn't stop smiling.

"One thing though, Richard: we can't tell anyone else. I was told not to say a word to anyone but my husband and immediate family."

It turns out that Richard was actually much more cautious than I was. Every day he would come in for either lunch or dinner and I would sit and talk to him about the show because he knew the show like no one else I knew. If I would talk a little too loud he would say, "Shhh! You never know who could be listening!" But I have to say that Richard really was just as excited as I was.

Two

Boston

Two weeks went by and it was time for my interview in Boston at CBS Studios. As the time approached I had become restless. I couldn't sleep. I'd sometimes get up and go for a run in the middle of the night! It was two of the most agonizing weeks of my life and had seemed more like two years!

But, if you can believe it, every day I became more excited than the day before. Of course I was a little nervous too, but who in their right mind wouldn't be? A path that led to one of my biggest long-time dreams had opened up. And it was up to me to find my way there.

I was so excited about the interview that all I could think about at first was getting in the best shape of my life and winning this thing. I had gotten to the point where I already believed that I just had to win, and the first thing I could think to do to prepare for *Survivor* was to exercise my body.

But when my thoughts turned toward the meeting itself I couldn't even form a picture in my mind of how it would be—to be honest I really didn't know what to expect.

So in order to feel in control of the situation I had tried to visualize what I was going to say while I was riding around in my car every day. I was trying to predict the questions they were going to ask me and I practiced answering every question I could possibly think of. Here are a handful that I thought they might ask me:

"If you won Sue, what would you do with the million dollars?"

"What do you think you can bring to *Survivor*?"

"How will your family feel having you gone for two months?"

"Do you think you have what it takes to be the Ultimate *Survivor*?"

"Is there anything you wouldn't do to win the game?"

"How do you feel about being stuck on an Island with 15 people you have never met?"

"What annoys you about other people?"

"Why do you think you could win this game?"

"Why did you pick a tube of red lipstick to bring as your luxury item?"

"What is your biggest fear?"

"What is your strategy to win *Survivor*?"

But let's face it: no matter how much you practice for something like that you're never prepared for the actual questions!

When the morning of August 8th arrived I woke up full of energy. I felt like a million bucks. I was in the best shape of my life (and that's saying something since I was a star swimmer for my high school when I was 18!). I had my hair all dolled-up, pulled up and twisted in the back. And of course I just happened to have had it colored the day before. I'm sure up until now you all thought I was a natural blonde. Sorry to dispel that myth!

I had my nails done. My legs looked like those of a twenty year old. I was tanned. I was feeling good. I wore a short, size four jean skirt with a tucked-in white fitted blouse from the Limited, and of course my four inch leather heels. Do you think that was why they would later call me Barbie? But that's okay because I know that I may look like Barbie, but Babe: don't ever judge a book by its cover!

And then I was off to Boston and CBS' Studio. I used MapQuest to print out the route for my trip, got in my car and headed out.

I was playing great music that I'd brought along for the occasion to motivate myself: *Ain't No Mountain High Enough*, *The Worlds Greatest*, Dan Hartman's *Instant Replay*, and ELO's *Hold on Tight to your Dream*. It was a great ride down! Despite my anxiety, I was having the time of my life. You know how you feel when you're in total control of the whole situation? Like when you're on an interview for a really great job but you're happy with the one you already have? Nothing feels better!

And then, too quickly it seemed, the ride was over and I had arrived in Cambridge Massachusetts. I looked to the left and there it was: a great big building with CBS STUDIOS emblazoned on the side. I was thinking, *How cool is this?* I parked my car in the studio lot and walked around to the front of the building. There was a serious security area at the entrance—armed guards and metal detectors like I was getting on a plane. Once through security I stopped at the front desk and told them who I was there to see.

I had been told what to say when I got there. I was not supposed to say anything about *Survivor*. So I walked in and said "Hi, I'm Sue Pollard and I'm here to see Martha Fainberg." They told me to have a seat and that someone would be right with me. So I sat and waited.

A million thoughts were going through my head. So I focused on trying to remember everything Martha had said in preparing for today's meeting. For example, she had told me how to dress. She had said to dress casually—as though I were going to meet a friend, so I did just that. I remember her saying that this was not a job interview and that they just wanted to get to know me face to face. But it sure felt like a job interview—or even worse, because it was more personal: a job interview where I wasn't being judged on my experience and background, but actually upon who I *am*.

As if to confirm my fears, Martha drove the point home: "Sue, there is no way to prepare for this interview. So just be yourself." So I was going to do just that.

What else had she said? Oh yes, that the interview was going to be videotaped. They had sent me a release form that I had to sign. And one last thing I could remember was that Martha had also asked me to bring my passport. This time, as I sat in the lobby of CBS Studios in Cambridge, without checking again (for what would have been the umpteenth time), I knew that I had.

At one point a gentlemen came down in the elevator and walked out right in front of me. I couldn't help but think that he must be one of the other 400 contestants as well.

But after only a few more minutes wait a woman came down to get me.

"Are you Sue Pollard?"

"Yes."

"Come with me."

A woman of few words! Fine by me—as long as they weren't expecting the same from me! Off we went to the elevator.

On the way up she told me to be myself.

"If you swear, swear. Just be yourself."

I nodded my head.

"Are you excited?" she asked.

"Very much!" She had no idea! I wondered how many people she had already escorted—and wondered if they were as nervous and excited as I was. I wasn't *worried*, really. I was confident that I would be able to sell them on myself. But I was anxious. I had no idea what to expect.

When we got off the elevator we walked straight down the hall to about the fifth room on the right. The girl who was escorting me knocked and the door opened to reveal a rather ordinary looking conference room. There was a table, some chairs, and a few fake plants here and there. The only element of the room that would have seemed out of place, in any other office building for any other company I'd ever visited, was the enormous production camera.

Martha introduced herself to me. She was about 5'6" tall. She was pretty, with dark brown hair and was very busty. She was nice but she kept to the point.

I learned later that Martha was one of Mark Burnett's more trusted leaders and that she had a great deal to do with the candidates who were ultimately selected to participate on the show. But at the time she was the only face and voice of the business-side of *Survivor* that I knew.

A gentleman put a lapel microphone on me and I remember distinctly that he was not shy in asking me to unbutton my blouse a little so he could put on the microphone.

They asked if I was ready and then they started in with the questions. The camera was rolling.

The Alternate Survivor

They started by asking me to tell them a little bit about myself. No problem there. I'm not afraid to talk and it helped me shake my nervousness to tell them about myself. And when I would say something funny the three in the room laughed in all the right places—so that helped too!

Then they asked other questions like would I get naked on national TV? No. Do I believe in open marriages? No. They asked about my personal life, my family, and my goals and why I thought I would be a good contestant on *Survivor*. And then Martha asked, "Sue, what if we made you famous?"

The answer came easily for me—even though it was one I hadn't prepared for. "I haven't thought about it but if you did, that would be awesome. But becoming famous? Isn't that something you do yourself? If you've got it, you've got it! And I know that one day I will be famous probably because of some crazy thing I do on my own!"

Little did I know at the time that it would be for challenging Mark Burnett!

Martha shrugged her shoulders and I went on.

"I think that becoming famous can be a head game for most people. I don't really care about the whole celebrity thing. I just want to have fun and do some great things for my family and for people who need it."

All three people in the room looked at me and smiled. I don't remember the guy's name in the room but he said "That's cool". A few minutes later the questions were over. I was done.

I hadn't thought it would go so fast and it surprised me. Trying to stall what had seemed to go too quickly I asked Martha what had gotten me this far in the *Survivor* process.

"What do you think?"

"My video?"

"Yes we loved your energy and you are very charismatic and we feel you fit the part we're looking for".

That was it. She seemed to want to move things along and before I could ask another question she hurried me out.

"Thanks, Sue. If we want to pursue this with you we will call you in a couple of weeks!"

The Alternate Survivor

On my way out the door I gave them one of my Suzipoo postcards that said "rock on" because they had said they'd loved my speech from the video. I left the room thinking that they were nice people. But man, were they really on a mission to get a job done!

As I walked toward the elevator I felt a bit let down, or at least a lot less confident, and a little off-balance. The meeting was so short. And I'd hardly had a chance to get comfortable. What was up with that? And they had been so hurried and efficient. I couldn't tell whether they were just trying to do their job as quickly as possible—because they had so many other people to interview, or whether they were doing it on purpose. Maybe they just didn't want me to know where I stood. Then a third possibility occurred to me the more I thought about it. And I wondered if, once they had met me, they had just decided that I probably wasn't a fit so they had cut short the interview.

The ride home from Boston was a difficult one because, for me, the worst part of a situation like that was not knowing what was going to happen. I am the type of person that is usually in control of my next move. And I really didn't like the fact that I had no control over whether I was going to be selected for *Survivor*. But, as if I had a choice, I went along with it and waited two very long weeks.

###

Well, the two weeks were up. It was August 24, 2002 and I had a school board meeting that night.

That whole day, and during the entire meeting that night my mind was thinking, *Okay the two weeks are up and I haven't gotten a phone call.* After the meeting I drove to my restaurant and pulled into the parking lot. My daughter Lauren was standing outside with a smile from one ear to the other.

"Mom, they called."

"What did they say, Lauren?" My heart was in my throat but her smile seemed to be a good sign.

"Ask Dad." She seemed to be wrestling with wanting to tell me herself.

So I went into the restaurant and took my husband aside. Despite my anxiousness I had to be discreet. After all, at this point I had only told my husband and my two daughters Miranda and Lauren (and of course Richard—without whom none of this would have been happening!). And the show had made a really big deal about the secrecy. I ran up the stairs where my husband was waiting for me. He was smiling. I begged him to tell me what they said. "Martha just said for you to call her." So Bob, Miranda, Lauren and I closed my office door and I called.

"Hello."

"Hi Martha, this is Sue Pollard."

"Hi! Sue, you made the final cut! You're coming to Los Angeles!"

I couldn't believe it! My dream of making it on national TV had come true.

I remember telling Martha, "I promise you I will make you proud of the decision you made by picking me." Her response was, "I have no doubt in my mind that you will do just that!" Again she told me she would send me all the information, and my e-ticket for the flight, and the hotel info, etc. I remember thanking her at least ten times. I hung the phone up and started crying with joy.

My family came over immediately and hugged me because they were so happy for me. One of my biggest dreams was about to happen.

The thought that I had made the cut from thousands to 38 contestants was unbelievable. I was so excited I couldn't contain myself. I was going to get my chance to show the world who I was, to show them my tenacity and my willpower. And I loved the fact that I would prove that it doesn't matter if you're 25, 35, 45 or even 55; if you've got it going on, you'll always have it going on! Here, finally, was my chance to "ROCK ON" in a *really* big way.

We chose not to tell our son Justin who was only nine at the time because we didn't want to upset him. We decided to wait until we thought the time was right. This was August 24th and I was leaving on September 9th. And what a long two weeks it was! I was dying to tell my friends but I didn't because CBS was so adamant in reminding me that I couldn't tell anyone. My anniversary was on September 8th. At the time I'd been married for 22 years. My husband and I went out to celebrate our anniversary and we also talked about my making it on *Survivor*. We both had our reservations about it.

The Alternate Survivor

Our biggest reservation was that my husband Bob would have to take care of everything—especially the kids. We both are very dedicated to our children but the fact that he had to do it all by himself for 40 days was crazy! I never missed my kids sports and I am also very involved with their school work. And Bob worked full time. It would be a pretty challenging 40 days for him, I knew. But then, it wasn't just the kids, either: I had always handled all the finances and shopping for our household, too. And, in my absence, Bob would just have to do it all.

As for us, Bob and I being apart was O.K. because we have a very strong relationship. We love each other very much and we believe in each other. He supports me in whatever I do. He knew I was going. And he knew that when I left I had a game to win, and I wasn't coming home without the million dollars!

Being away from our family that long was going to be rough—on me, on Bob, and on the kids. I knew I would miss my family. But when I thought about actually being on *Survivor* I was so excited for the challenge and for the rush!

Three

Los Angeles

The morning of September 9th arrived and I had to be at the airport at eleven a.m. I took my kids to school. Justin must have hugged me twenty times still thinking I was going to LA for *business stuff*.

My husband drove me to the airport. The whole time we talked about this chance of a lifetime. I will say that a part of me was a little nervous. After all, I still knew very little about the show. And here I was at the airport alone, leaving my family for eleven days. This was just the beginning, of course. If I were selected, I would be away for 40 days straight! I got a little emotional. I called my mom and said goodbye. She had no idea that I was even going to L.A. let alone that I was going to be a finalist on *Survivor*. I told her it was for business, of course. She told me to be careful. If she only knew!

I remember waiting at the airport to board the plane like it was yesterday. It was September 9th, 2002—only two days away from the one year anniversary of the tragedy of 9/11. I couldn't stop thinking about flying to California along the same route that the flight was supposed to take from Boston to L.A. just a year earlier.

I wasn't afraid to fly in the traditional sense. And I wasn't *really* afraid that another act of terrorism would occur which involved my flight. So I tried to ignore whatever anxiety I was feeling and just put myself in God's hands, trusting that I would be okay. But I couldn't help thinking about what the passengers of those airplanes must have been thinking on that horrible day in our country's history.

The Alternate Survivor

Looking back now, almost five years later, I still think about the tragedy of 9/11 and I remember so well what it was like to live in this country at that time. We all came together as Americans. We felt a sense of common suffering and we looked to each other to endure it. As a people we were bound together by participating in a shared tragedy. And as fellow survivors of that tragedy, many of us shed our self-centered outlook on life.

There was a palpable sense of community that reminded me of what our country was like 50 or 100 years ago. All of the American flags and the home-town parades made us feel good. All of the renewed respect everyone seemed to feel for our veterans, and our firemen and our policemen was a sign that we were aware once again that there was a world that existed beyond our front door, outside of our car's windshield, and beyond the office building in which we worked.

Unfortunately, for too many of us, these feelings would prove to be all too temporary. I think it's a shame that we haven't been able to hold onto that surge of patriotism and goodwill toward our neighbors. I really, sincerely wish we could bring it back. I'd like to think that, if not as a nation, we still keep that sense of unity and community alive in us as individuals. And I believe that as individuals, we have the power to bring it back for the whole country once again. It shouldn't require an act of terrorism to inspire it. One person at a time, I believe we can inspire our own communities and touch the world around us. I believe we should all try to do good deeds in the world and show people that we care about more than ourselves. And I think that such actions can and will inspire those around us to do the same.

But I'll step off my soap-box now and get back to the story!

My e-ticket was waiting for me just as Martha said it would be and I boarded the plane. I was so excited. After I was settled into my seat I couldn't help but wonder what everyone else was doing on this plane? I wanted to yell out "I'm a finalist for *SURVIVOR*! Do any of you realize this?"

Instead, I tried to sit still for the five-hour trip and read my book on surviving in the wilderness. I had trouble keeping focus. Were there other hopefuls on board? I kept looking around and checking everybody out. A handful seemed possible but most seemed far too "normal" to be *Survivor* candidates. I kept going back to my book, trying to distract myself from the stray thoughts about being on *Survivor*, and about being on television.

While in flight I had another moment where thoughts of 9/11 crossed my mind and I've got to admit that I did take a look around at the other passengers. I usually don't think too much about dying because I live life every day like it's my last and I pray that I last every day I'm given. I feel that when my time comes, and when my life on earth is over, that there's not much I can do about it anyway. As a Christian, I'm not afraid to die because I know that the Lord already has a plan for me. But, all of that said, I will also say that I was relieved when we landed safely!

Before I knew it, the pilot was saying we would be landing in Los Angeles in approximately 20 minutes. My stomach knotted up. All of a sudden I realized that the excitement had been building up in me during the flight. I was more excited than I could ever have imagined.

We landed and the mundane activities of having to retrieve my own bags and get a cab took away a little of my anxiety. I felt grateful that there was something for me to do.

I had orders to take a taxi to Santa Monica. The address was for the Doubletree Hotel. I was told to get a receipt and that they would pay for the taxi. So I did.

The cab driver didn't talk to me at all. In fact I don't even know if he spoke English! I remember asking him about the smoke in the hills far away. He didn't seem to understand me, but I found out later that my trip had happened while the California hills were in the middle of one of the worst years for wildfires in more than 50 years. I kept the rest of my questions to myself and just accepted that he would take me where I needed to go.

As I rode, I looked out with amazement at L.A. The traffic was crazy and the freeway was just packed! I remember seeing cars and even fast food places I had never even heard of. Compared with southern Maine this was like another planet—and the smoke in the hills just added to the surrealism of the ride. What strange and frantic world had I stepped into? Then, before I knew it, we were at the Doubletree Hotel.

I checked in quickly—eager to begin my adventure.

I had been told that as soon as I got there I was to call them and confirm that I was there. I got to the room and I looked out the window. Right across the street from me was the beautiful Pacific Ocean. My first thoughts were that this was going to be an unbelievable ten days. No laundry, no responsibilities, not having to work 18 hours a day. And I couldn't wait to get to that beach! Well it turns out that I never did get to swim in that ocean, or set foot on that beautiful beach. Mark Burnett and his crew had other plans for me.

I didn't even unpack my bag before I called the number that I had been given. I believe I spoke to a woman named Ellen. She said, "Come down to room such and such and I will give you your instructions." There was no "How was your trip?" or any small-talk whatsoever. I felt like I was in a spy movie, or something!   Just "come down to my room". So I went down to her room and I knocked on the door.

"Come in."

I walked into her room all smiles, ready for my first human contact of the trip. But instead of a welcome or a "Congratulations for making it this far!" or more than even a cursory "hello" she began to lay down the ground rules.

"You cannot talk to anyone. If you see any of the other contestants you need to look away and do not talk to them. Do not, in fact, talk with anyone in this hotel."

She handed me a schedule:

Breakfast -- 7:30 A.M. to 8:00 A.M.

Lunch -- 1:30 to 2:15 P.M.

Workout time -- 4:30 to 5:30 P.M.

Dinner -- 7pm to 7:45pm P.M.

"You need to stay in your room until further notice."

It turns out I wasn't even allowed to speak to the woman who came in to clean my room (who, by the way, was the only company I had for ten days outside of the official *Survivor* "sessions"). Did I mention that I like people, and that I like to be social? Well I do—on both counts. And spending eleven days with such restrictions placed upon me was like a form of psychological torture. I actually wondered at various points if it truly were intentional because it affected me so strongly.

The woman continued, "If, for some reason, you miss one of these break times, then you'll have to do without. You will not have another opportunity. If, for any reason, your break is interrupted or missed—even if it is because we need you to meet with the producers and it is during one of your breaks—you will not receive another opportunity."

And then she was done. I was dismissed.

I was to return to my room.

I felt like I was in prison. Really, I did.

I walked back to my room, confused again. Was this any way to treat people that you were selecting to appear on your show? I didn't understand. Even now, having read Mark Burnett's books and understanding better what I think he was trying to do it's hard for me to look back on these days of confinement and see how they make sense. Okay, so I understand that he wanted us to keep the whole process a secret and that's why he told us not to talk to anyone. And he didn't want us to talk to each other because he wanted our first real "meetings" to be on film in the Amazon. I get it. But the rest of it? The isolation and the prison-like restrictions on my movement and behavior? I still can't help but wonder if that was one of our tests, too.

Back in my room I looked out the windows once again at the beautiful Pacific Ocean.

In my letter congratulating me they did say there would be some downtime and that I should bring something to do. But I never in my wildest dreams thought the down time would be for 21 hours a day for ten days!

If you knew me, you would realize that I felt like a caged lion in a very small box! I was beside myself. When it was time for me to go to breakfast, work out or do anything outside of my room, my hand was on the doorknob waiting for that clock to hit the correct time to go.

Another day went by where I could only get out of my room a few times a day. And then another. When I would leave my room I would try to look around and get the lay of the land. Because I couldn't talk to anyone, I felt like a complete outsider. I felt bold just by glancing at the other faces that I passed in the hall and in the common areas of the hotel. They had me so brainwashed that I was even nervous to give the hostess my ticket for the buffet we had every meal.

After a couple days I started to notice about 10 to 12 other people sitting alone at their own tables in the cafeteria. I thought that they looked like I felt. They weren't saying a word. They looked out of place and off-balance. They had to be the other contestants. Now I know and recognize that they were Butch, Deana, Christy, Matthew, Dan & Jenna. And, of course, there were others who I probably will never know.

After another day or two it became kind of funny because we might accidentally meet eyes with each other and then have to look away. It was only a matter of time before we all knew why we were there. One time at the food buffet I was inches behind Butch and just being polite as I am, I reached for something and said, "Excuse me." He said, "Certainly." And all I could think at the time was "Gee, I hope no one saw me say that!" They had me feeling that crazy!

A few other incidents happened when I went to work out everyday. We were in a workout room that was maybe 25'X25'—not very big. There were three stationary bikes in a row. I was on one. Matthew was right next to me--I mean, we were just inches from one another. And Deana was running on the elliptical trainer. There was also a young blonde guy, who obviously didn't make it either, who would eat and work out at the same time I did. When our time was up we would go back to our rooms and sit. And sit. And sit.

On day three Martha came to my room. I was excited to see a familiar face and you can't even know how glad I was for the company—not to mention the simple distraction from my isolation! She was there to tell me that the next day I would be meeting Jeff Probst. I said, "Who's that?" Martha said, "The host!" I remember looking at her like I was stupid and said, "I thought his name was John." She said, "Jeff, John. Oh, it's just a syllable." So I simply said, "Okay." It was a simple mistake on my part, but it just goes to show you how little I really knew about the show that I was trying out for! I wasn't even enough of a fan to remember the host's name correctly!

When I went to the interview I really wasn't nervous. I was just happy to get out of my room and have the chance to *talk*! I walked in and the room was darkened somewhat and there were about eighteen people seated around me in a horseshoe. They had me sit in the opening of the "U". Nobody was saying anything and I suppose they probably wanted to see what I would do when they put me in such an uncomfortable position as the focus of attention. Or maybe they expected me to recognize Jeff Probst. Like so many things about the *Survivor* experience I'm really not sure I can guess at the "reasons" why things were done the way they were. But I wasn't going to be intimidated and once I was seated I just looked around at them. When the silence continued and it was clear they were waiting for me to say something I tried to be funny and light-hearted and I just smiled and said "Hi"--and nothing more. Then, without any introduction or small-talk--as was so characteristic of the entire experience--the questions started.

The first couple of questions seemed to be the same ones that were asked at my first interview in Boston and others were repetitious, as well.

Would you get naked on national TV?

"No, I just wouldn't. I'm a mom of three, Sunday School Superintendent, chairperson of the school board and I do not feel it would represent what I stand for. When I was 21 and single? Maybe."

Do I believe in open marriages?

"No, I don't."

How would you characterize yourself?

"I'm very outgoing, tenacious, caring, aggressive, loyal, athletic, and of course sexy! Ha!"

What kind of person are you?

"Let's put it this way, if someone is an idiot, hurts me or my family, is always condescending, I'll screw him or her to the wall. *But,* if someone is trying their best and is a good person I will carry them over that finish line!" I remember looking at Mark Burnett as he nodded with a smile.

If you were stranded on a desert island, who would you not *want to be with?*

"Martha Stewart. Nothing personal but I find her rather boring and self-centered." Now, of course, I realize that Mark Burnett respects Ms. Stewart and has since done business with her. Whoops! But I did say that my comments weren't personal!

Who would you want to be stuck on an island with?

"Two people. First, Kevin James because I think he is hilarious."

One of the producers chimed in, "Well he's really not that funny."

"Well, we all have our own opinions, don't we?" Maybe I was a little too confident in front of them. Again, I was just being myself. "And the other person I would want to be on an island with is Steven Segal because you never know when you really might have to kick some ass!"

That one brought more laughter.

What is your strategic plan to win Survivor?

"I'm going to start by just being me. I'm going to try to have fun, work hard, and have a positive attitude. And when we're down to the final four I'm going to kick their ASS!"

They all laughed. I thought I'd scored a good answer with that one.

What are you most proud of?

"Obviously my children and my husband are my world, but one thing I am very proud of is how I went from being an average, distracted student to becoming Chairperson of my local School Board."

"I grew up in a large family where my mom and dad both worked a lot. School was tough for me. I really never had the help I needed. And I'm not trying to put the blame on my parents because they did the best they could for me—providing for and loving all five of us very much. They did their best and I am who I am today because of their hard work, and their loyalty to each other and to the family. My mom has only an eighth grade education and is smarter and greater than any one person I know! My dad died at 58 with cancer. But I can only hope I have the loving relationship my parents had."

"I remember one of the ways my parents could have helped me during my own school years. Teachers and administrators always intimidated me. And, even as an adult, as my children got older and I became more involved in their school system, I realized that I was still intimidated by them. So I thought *what better way to get over this intimidation than to run for the school board?* So I ran. And since I am such an outgoing and well-known person in my community, and I always treat people with generosity and respect, I won easily.

"And here I am today: Chair of the school board. I'm not being sent to the Superintendent's office for discipline. I'm basically the Superintendent's boss. How far you can come when you want something and you don't let the word 'no' get in your way.

"I remember standing in front of over 200 teachers and all the administrators giving the opening remarks for the new school year. At the end of the speech I said, 'You know that kid in your classroom who is talking when they shouldn't be, doesn't pass their homework in on time, and maybe has a little extra energy? Well don't just quit on that kid because she might one day grow up and be the owner of her own successful company and CHAIR OF THE SCHOOL BOARD!' Like any speech I give-- whether it's to the graduating class or to the teachers on opening day--my closing remark is 'Always Rock On!' Well the whole room clapped for at least five minutes. So many people gave me a pat on the back after the opening and smiled and said 'That was great, Sue!'"

"So, to make a long story short, that accomplishment is one that I am very proud of. And that speech I gave was a big milestone for me."

There were a lot of nodding heads and smiles as I finished. I think they liked the story. And I thought it was a good sign.

At the end of the interview I asked if I could ask a question and they said sure. I asked who actually created the show and they all looked over to Mark Burnett and said that Mark was the creator of *Survivor*. I remember Mark modestly trying to dodge the compliment by saying that really it was a gentleman by the name of Charlie Parsons.

But the producers and all the people in the room said, "No, it was Mark Burnett who came up with this genius idea." I asked if I could shake his hand. He smiled and stood up. I walked over to him, shook his hand, looked him straight in the eyes and said, "You're a genius."

From that moment I knew one day somehow I would have something to do with this man and I still believe *Survivor* is the way that I will.

Three or four days went by and my hotel phone rang. It was Ellen telling me to be in a certain room at two o'clock. So the time came and I went. I got there and in the room were at least 30 people, all facing the wall getting ready to take a test. It was a three-hour test with over 400 questions. I remember the instructor saying that there were no right or wrong answers, and that we should just answer each question regarding how we would handle a certain situation as truthfully as we could. It was obviously some type of personality or character profile. After completing the test we were told to go back to our rooms.

The next day I was called to meet with the psychologist to get the results of my test. He said I had to be one of the most optimistic people he'd ever met. I smiled! He then went on and explained the test to me. I had scored very high, especially when it came to optimism and being a go-getter.

With all of that said, I felt pretty good. And I thought the producers would be impressed. I guess they must have been because I was called back for a second interview.

In the beginning I had been told that if they felt I was not what they were looking for I would be sent home in the first few days. Going into my 8th day I was starting to feel pretty positive that I was going to be on *Survivor* 6. Also, at least twice a day I would have a visit from Martha, Jocelyn and others from the casting crew. They would stop by and talk a little to see how I was doing, etc. I would love to have them stop by mostly for the company.

Anyway, getting back to the second interview . . .

It was crazy. I was told what I should wear and not wear. I was told not to wear my high leather sandals. I asked why not? One of the responses was

"Well Sue you look too much like a Barbie." I said, "Barbie? Why is my hair too blonde? Are my boobs too big? And for that matter, if I were Barbie I would kick Ken's ASS!" She laughed and said, "You're a piece of work!"

I also told them not to ever judge a book by its cover. Because even with my short shorts, my high heels and great legs and my voluptuous body, I still have what it takes to be the ultimate *Survivor*!

So I got ready for my second interview. At this point I really think they had narrowed it down to the top 25 or 30. That was my gut feeling. Anyway, I was told to be at a certain room at a certain time. When I arrived I saw Ellen. She looked at me and put her finger to her mouth basically telling me not to speak. She put me and seven other women in a van. Among those girls were Jenna, Heidi, Janet and Christy—who sat so close to me that our arms were touching. (They had us so crazy over the 'no speaking or interacting with the other candidates' rules that I have moments to this day where I vaguely wonder whether that might be the reason why I didn't make it!) There were also four other women in the van. So, of course, I thought this was our second interview and this must be the eight women who had made it. It just seemed logical at the time.

The women were of mixed age: some were young and some middle-aged. When we arrived at CBS studios, again we were told not to speak. "Don't even cough." So all of us in the van got out like ducklings. We followed the leader and were brought into a large conference room. We all sat around a big table. They brought us lunch and we watched TV while waiting. We were given a speech in which we were told that we might go in for an interview and we might not. We were also told that either way it didn't necessarily mean anything.

"You may have already made it. Or maybe you're just on the edge and they need to see you one more time."

On the way into the conference room, once we went through security, we walked by a group of eight men including Butch, Matthew, Dan and others. I do not remember seeing Rob, although I wished I had because he seemed like a fun guy. Martha called me out into the hall right before I went into the room for my last interview. She said, "Suzi, I don't know what you're doing, but keep it up because they love you." So the door opened and I went in for my last interview with the producers. Mark Burnett was sitting straight in front of me.

This interview seemed more relaxed than the last one. I remember walking into the room and one of the women said, "Well, Sue—are you ready to kick some ASS?" She was obviously a loud and outgoing troublemaker—I liked her! And I almost shouted through my smile in response: "You bet I am!"

The atmosphere in the room remained very casual throughout the entire interview and I truly felt like I had made it. They asked how my children and husband were going to deal with me being gone. They asked me if I had any regrets or second thoughts about participating. I also remember someone asking me what my biggest fear was. My response was that I wasn't afraid of anything or anyone but if I had one fear it would be snakes. I hate snakes. But I told them I would just have to deal with them if I had to.

Other than that they went through the same questions they had before: Are you sure you wouldn't get naked on national TV? Would you miss your family? To that last question I told them that of course I would miss my family but I had known what I was signing up for and I was ready to go!

The interview went great. I truly thought I was going to be selected for *Survivor*. After our interviews were over we all piled back in the van and headed back to our hotel. Again we received the same lecture: no talking, no gestures, and no nothing. By this point I could recite the rules. We got back to the hotel and went back to our rooms.

Once again, it was the same program: *Stay in our rooms. Only come out when you are told.*

That night I remember going down for dinner and the lobby was full of people and one of the casting crew met me. When I came out of the elevator he said "Sue, follow me. You're too close to making it. Go back upstairs until the lobby calms down." So I did. About one hour later I was told I could go down for dinner. When I went to get in the elevator the door opened and two of the *Survivor* contestants that I had seen all week were in there.

The three of us just turned our backs to each other. When the elevator stopped we got out and went to dinner. As always, we sat at our tables alone, always being watched by the casting crew. They would walk around the cafeteria with walkie-talkies—like prison guards, or Secret Service agents—informing each other exactly what was going on, exactly what we were doing and when we would leave. They watched our every move.

At this point I had been there for nine days and the next day I was going home. That night at around 6:30 I got a phone call, I believe from Ellen, saying, "Sue, guess what? You've made it to the top twenty. You need to come down and get your shots and give us your passport. I'll call you when it's time for you to come downstairs. Are you excited?"

"I can't believe it!"

I really felt I had made it! Well an hour went by. And then another. And then another. Before I knew it, it was 1:00 A.M. I was trying so hard not to fall asleep when the phone rang.

"Hi Suzi, come up to the 8th floor: room 812."

So off I went. I knocked on the door. Jocelyn answered, "Come in."

There was a doctor there with six needles lined up, who explained what they were: A shot for malaria, typhoid fever, etc. The doctor said, "I will give you three in each arm." Being the hotshot that I am I said, "No, put them all in one arm. I'm a *Survivor!*"

Well, to say the least, he did. As I winced from each needle, Jocelyn was so cute. She said to me "Do you want me to hold your hand?" I said, "Sure." Each shot they gave me stung more than the one before it and Jocelyn kept saying to me: "Just think of all the Suzipoo you can sell once you're on *Survivor*". That made me smile. Jocelyn asked me for my passport and told me she would call me within two weeks to let me know if I had made the cut from twenty to sixteen.

Well, come on! After what I had been through I was sure I was going on *Survivor*. So back to my room I went. I had already been given my itinerary for my flight home. I was to leave the hotel at 5:30 on the morning of Thursday, September 19th—the first day that *Survivor* Thailand would air.

I was ready to go home and see my family. Even though most of my time had been spent being idle, and I'd been going stir-crazy from it, it had still been an exhausting ordeal. And I was also eager to watch *Survivor* Thailand when I got home because here I was going on the show and I probably had watched the show only three or four times up to this point.

I understand that there have been other contestants who weren't necessarily fans of the show when they decided to apply to be on it. And in at least one case I believe the girl from Maine named Zoë had never watched the show even *once* before making it onto *Survivor*. As for myself: of course I didn't think it was a requirement that I was a fan or knew every episode of the show, but I admit that I was curious—and the closer I came to being on the show the more I wanted to know about it. And, of course, I couldn't ask any of my friends who were die-hard fans about the show because we were told not to tell anyone—including brothers, sisters and parents!

So I got on the plane. And, of course, there was a delay so when I finally landed in Boston it was 1:30 in the morning. I was beat, but I realized that I had better get used to that feeling if I were going to be traveling to the Amazon for *Survivor* 6.

Four

Back to Reality

I was home again. And I tried to get back into my routine. As you might guess, after the experience in California, nothing was *normal*. A single thought ran through my mind constantly: "I'm going on *Survivor*!" And I so much wanted to tell *everyone* that I had just spent ten days with the casting crew for *Survivor*, Jeff Probst and Mark Burnett. I don't know about you, but that's not *normal* in my life! All my friends were asking how my business trip was and all I could say was just "Great." Period.

So a week went by and every day at this point I was expecting that phone call. Nothing. Once again the waiting was torture. I was so distracted— even more than usual! And I was torn between my trademark confidence and self-assurance and the growing knot in my stomach that had me wondering if the delay was a bad sign, and that I'd have been told already if I were definitely going.

Then finally, exactly two weeks to the day on October 3rd, 2002 I was at a parent/teacher conference. I came home and there was a message. "Hi Sue. It's Jocelyn. Give me a call." I called right away. No answer. I tried five more times. Nothing. So I went to bed and didn't sleep much that night. Remembering that there was a three hour time difference, I called her at eleven a.m. my time or eight a.m. Jocelyn's time. She answered. I said, "Hi Jocelyn. It's Sue."

I could tell by the tone of her voice it wasn't good.

"Sue, I'm sorry but you didn't make it."

"What? I can't believe it."

"I know. You were so close."

Honestly, I thought at this point that they were still testing me. I really couldn't believe I didn't make it.

I had gone from this unbelievable high to a low and a sense of loss like I truly have never felt. I just couldn't understand it and couldn't come to grips with it.

"What went wrong? How could you not take me? Did I do something wrong?"

The whole time I was there all I heard was how much they liked my energy, my "can do" attitude, that I was so upbeat, and the fact that I was on the school board because of my love for kids. I also remember in one of the interviews saying how cool it would be that I am on the school board and always teaching kids never to give up and always to ROCK ON! This was such a great opportunity for me to prove to them that you should never quit. They would be able see that I truly meant it!

Jocelyn talked to me for a few minutes and said, "Sue don't give up."

We said goodbye. I remember it like it was yesterday. I just sat back in my chair in my office and looked at the ceiling with dismay. I'd put so much time and emotional energy into this thing. How was it possible that they didn't pick me? It was so frustrating that such a thing was happening to me that I had so little control over! I'd always been able to make my own way before, and never been so reliant upon other people for my own success. It was going to make me go crazy thinking about it.

So I called her right back and I said, "Jocelyn I'm not giving up!" She was so cute. She said, "Sue I'll tell you right now, do you know Tina Wesson from *Survivor: Outback*? Well she missed the cut by one also. The last minute, for whatever unknown reason, one of the other *Survivor*s couldn't make the trip and Tina was called. She joined at the last minute and ended up winning *Survivor: Outback*."

So I still had that glimpse of hope. It wasn't even two hours later when three of my best friends called me: the friends I had given for references. My dear friend Sharma called me and said, "What are you up to now? I just got a call asking a lot of things about you. The questions were: *How long had I known Sue? What kind of person is she? Does she drink? How responsible is she? What is the craziest thing you know she has done?* They had asked all kinds of crazy questions and *not* the questions you would expect someone to ask unless they might be trying out for something out of the ordinary."

Then the Superintendent of Schools called me and told me he had just had this strange conversation with a man asking a lot of personal questions about me. He answered them knowing he had written me a letter of recommendation for *Survivor* but not knowing when I asked him to write it that it was such a "top secret" process.

Finally, the next day Richard Payeur came into the restaurant with a big smile on his face. (And remember that he was one of the very few people I had confided in, since he was the one who had encouraged me to apply in the first place!) He approached me and told me that he had just gotten a phone call asking all kinds of questions about me. Questions like: *What is the craziest thing you have known Sue Pollard to do? Does she drink? How long have you known Sue?* Basically the questions they had just asked Sharma and Ed McDonough the Superintendent. I knew it wasn't over like Jocelyn had said—or why else would they be pursuing me?

So after getting all these phone calls I figured they must be doing a background investigation on me. And my hopes went through the ceiling. I am going, I thought! Or was this just another crazy way of screwing with my mind? I wondered if all of the other applicants were undergoing the same drama—and this was just a way to keep the contestants guessing until the very last moment so they didn't have enough time to mentally prepare themselves. Or maybe it was so people didn't have a chance to blow the secret and tell others what they were up to. Looking back I think it may have been both. Mark Burnett seems to really care about the "reality" of his shows. And keeping people on the edge and unprepared seems *right* up his alley. And, of course, the secrecy would be important to him for similar reasons—he would want the audience at home to be as surprised with everything as the contestants themselves were.

So a week went by and at this point my emotions were completely shot. I didn't know if I was going to be in Maine next week or in some crazy faraway place!

Nine days passed. I had just come home from a funeral. A high school student had been killed in an automobile accident.

It was a young girl. She was a junior in high school and hadn't had her license very long. And she was an only child. Her girlfriend, who had been a passenger when she had the accident, was in critical condition—and thankfully pulled through. I remember so clearly being at her wake. It was a closed casket with a beautiful picture of her on top and her surfboard and some stuffed animals in front. I love to surf with my kids so when I walked into that funeral home and saw that surfboard it just really hit home.

My daughter Miranda sat next to me at the funeral. I remember taking her hand and just thanking God for her safety. But my heart was broken for the girl's parents. They seemed inconsolable. They sobbed during the entire service. Afterward, I remember hugging them both and saying how sorry I was. I had not known the girl who was killed but had gone to lend my support from the community to this poor family. How impossible it must have been for that couple to move on from the loss of their only child.

The whole time I was sitting at that funeral I reflected on how lucky I was to have my own children safe. I can't even let myself imagine how such a loss would affect me. At the time, my not making *Survivor* had faded into insignificance. I felt guilty, in fact, for having allowed myself to be so disappointed over something that, in the big scheme of things, shouldn't have been such a priority.

That afternoon my daughter Miranda and I came home. The phone rang. I looked on Caller ID and it read 'private caller'. That is what always came up when Jocelyn or Martha or any of the casting crew called.

"Hello?"

"Hi Sue. It's Jocelyn."

"Hi." I had never expected to hear from her again.

"You need to get two more shots and get checked for HIV and Hepatitis B."

This was too much. First they made me wonder—no, in fact they TOLD ME OUTRIGHT that

I didn't make it! Then, all of sudden, they were telling me I needed more shots?! I couldn't contain myself: "Jocelyn, what's going on? Did I make it?"

"WELL, WHAT DO YOU THINK?"

Well if someone said that to you, tell me what would you think? Of course you'd feel just like I did: I thought I'd made it!

She went on to say that one of the women that had made the final cut had a medical situation that was most likely going to prevent her from making the show. I tried to get more information out of her but of course Jocelyn wouldn't give me any of the details.

So the next morning I got my shots and the results from my HIV test which were negative. I sent the results off with a pound of fudge and a music box that played *That's What Friends Are For*.

The next day I got an e-mail from Jocelyn, which I still have, saying thanks for getting us the results so quickly.

Well that was the last time I ever heard from her. I knew after two weeks went by, and the date that shooting was supposed to start had come and gone, that it was over and that I hadn't made it.

Did they put me on a roller coaster ride, or what?! Once I was convinced that it was truly over I called up my dear friend Richard Payeur and told him the whole story. He couldn't believe it. I remember him saying that all that I had gone through just wasn't right and that they should never have treated anyone the way they treated me. I think he felt bad that he had talked me into trying out for the show in the first place. But I will say that Richard knows me well and he knows I'm not a quitter. When this book is done, he'll smile and say he knew he picked the right girl for *Survivor*!

And in the end, if Mark Burnett truly is looking for the Ultimate *Survivor*: Well Mark, you found her!

I waited not-so-patiently for the first *Survivor* episode. Finally, in January of 2003, the TV guide came out and there they were.

I looked at each of them knowing that I had spent a somewhat surreal 10 days with most of them at a Doubletree hotel in Santa Monica. It was kind of cool that I actually knew them by face—even if I didn't know what their voices sounded like! And it was also interesting reading about each one of them.

And while the TV Guide inspired me, it just didn't give me enough information. And frankly, at this point I was a bit obsessed. So I went onto the CBS.com website and the section on Survivor and I read about each of the contestants there, too.

Every contestant's picture and profile also had a little camera icon next to their name. And when you clicked on the camera, it played a short video clip of each of them taken in their hotel rooms on their last night in United States.

It was actually a really cool feature. This is how it would work:

A cameraman and a woman would knock on the door and then walk into each contestant's hotel room and ask a handful of questions. You couldn't see either the woman or the cameraman who were doing the taping and asking the questions but I thought I recognized the voice as Jocelyn Green's. All of the videos were cool, but the one that really caught my attention was the one where Jocelyn entered Shawna Mitchell's room.

And the question itself that got my attention was the following:

"So Shawna, you almost didn't make the trip, huh? Breaking your toe almost was the end of your beginning of Survivor!"

Shawna went on to say "Yes, I'm very lucky that I pulled it together and got the okay from the doctor."

A big light went off in my head and I thought, *Shawna must have been the woman Jocelyn was talking to me about! The one that I was going to replace!* Can you believe it? That's just how close I actually was! I was going to go in place of Shawna because she had broken her toe!

But, even with the excitement of my discovery, the longer I looked at the site the more bummed out I became because I should have made it. The whole thing had been such an exercise in psychological warfare. And it seemed only fair that after such torture I would at least be able to say that it had been worth it because I'd been selected to participate in the show. But as it was I couldn't even justify the whole thing to myself because I felt so discarded and disappointed.

And when I watched the show I became even more frustrated. When Janet was whining to go home I just shook my head because no matter what, no matter how tough the situation seemed or how exhausted or how hungry I was, you would never see me whine about it! I had known what I was getting myself into and if you knew me you would know that when I make a decision there's no going back until the job is done!

So that was it, right? My bid to be on *Survivor* was over so I should just go back to my regular life and pretend that it never happened?

My heart said "I don't think so!", but what could I do? So I took the same approach I take when I'm selling for my business: I started writing letters to Mark Burnett via *Survivor*. According to the applicant agreement, once you make it as far as being a finalist in Los Angeles you cannot reapply to be on the show. But that wasn't going to stop me. I made Suzipoo postcards for Mark Burnett. In fact, to really show him my persistence, I sent him letters every week for a year. I guess you would have to know me. *No* was just not an option.

I mean, how could I get up and preach to the jr. high and all the high school kids telling them "When someone tells you "No" you say 'Yes I Can!'"? Or how could I tell them never to give up on their dreams if I did. Or that when you want something you let nothing get in your way--especially FEAR!

Okay. You're reading this book and probably thinking: *Sue, so what? So you didn't make it on Survivor. Get over it!* But I'm not done yet . . .

The Alternate Survivor

Thursday, July 18, 2002

Dear Applicant,

CONGRATULATIONS!!!!! You have been chosen for the second round of our selection process for "Survivor 6."

The date, time and location for your interview are on the attached page. Please note that the interview itself takes about fifteen minutes, but please allot for two hours, as there may be mechanical problems. All travel expenses for the interview are your responsibility.

The dress for the interview is casual. This is not a job interview; we just want to get to know you face to face. There is no way to prepare for the interview, just be yourself.

The interview will be videotaped, so we have enclosed a release form. Please read it, SIGN it and BRING it with you to the interview. You will also need to bring a copy of your valid passport if you did not have it at the time of your application.

Approximately fifty people will be invited to come to Los Angeles from about September 9th- 20th for final interviews with "Survivor" producers. Filming for the show will occur from October through mid-December 2002. These dates should be taken seriously; there will be no changes or exceptions. Please let us know if there is a conflict prior to your interview.

Please call Martha Fainberg at ████████ to confirm your interview date and time.

Best of luck.

Lynne Spiegel Spillman
Casting Director, Survivor

This is the letter telling me that I was going to LA!

Pollard & Berg

INDIVIDUAL REPORT

Cautionary Remarks:
This computerized report is meant to act as an interpretive aid and should not be used as the sole basis for placement, intervention, or other kinds of decision making. This report works best when combined with other sources of relevant information. The report is based on an algorithm that produces the interpretations most common for the scores that are obtained. Unusual interpretations must be explored with other instruments and on a case-by-case basis.

INTERPRETATION GUIDE FOR THE EQ-i COMPOSITE AND CONTENT SUBSCALE SCORES
The following sections describe the meaning of scores for the Total EQ-i Scale and each of the EQ-i content scales. In general, high scores identify areas of relative strength. Scores in the average range on these scales indicate satisfactory functioning and are scores that are obtained by the majority of those in the population who have taken the EQ-i. Low scores indicate areas that need to be improved in order to increase overall emotional and social intelligence. If all the scores are high or all the scores are low, it is useful to identify the scales with the highest and lowest scores; this will help pinpoint areas of relative strength or weakness.

TOTAL EQ SCALE SCORE (119):
The Total EQ indicates that, overall, emotional and social functioning is high. However, there are one or more areas that are not as high as the others. Clearly, these areas are compensated for by strengths in other areas and lead to an overall high EQ. Nonetheless, the identification of these growth areas can lead to even higher levels of emotional intelligence and even greater success in dealing with daily demands. A more detailed description of the EQ components is given in the next section.

INTRAPERSONAL EQ Scale Score (122):
This component of the Total EQ-i Score pertains to the assessment of the inner self. The subcomponents of the Intrapersonal EQ scale include Self-Regard, Emotional Self-Awareness, Assertiveness, Independence, and Self-Actualization.

The responses to items on the Total Intrapersonal scale are indicative of an individual who is in touch with her feelings, feels good about herself and about life in general. It is likely that Sue is independent, strong-minded, and able to express and convey feelings and ideas with confidence.

Self-Regard Subscale Score (119):
The responses to the Self-Regard scale indicate better than average self-regard, self-respect, self-confidence, and a person who has a good sense of who she is and who has positive feelings about life in general.

Emotional Self-Awareness Subscale Score (119):
The results indicate enhanced emotional self-awareness. Sue is in touch with her feelings and emotions, and usually knows what she is feeling and why. This individual is also comfortable expressing feelings to others.

Assertiveness Subscale Score (117):
The responses indicate an ability to express feelings and emotions. This individual is rarely self-conscious and can openly express feelings, thoughts, and beliefs in a constructive manner.

Independence Subscale Score (114):
The responses indicate an individual who is independent in her thinking and who also has a strong preference to act independently. These people may ask others for advice, but they rarely depend upon others to make important decisions for them (or in their lives). This individual prefers to be in charge rather than being under the supervision of someone else.

Self-Actualization Subscale Score (118):
Sue is achieving, or coming close to achieving, her full potential in most aspects of her life. This individual is probably deriving a great deal of enjoyment from life and is involved in pursuits that are meaningful, interesting and exciting for her.

The results from my personality test in LA (1 of 3).

94

The Alternate Survivor

INTERPERSONAL EQ SCALE SCORE(120):

This component of the Total EQ-i Scale taps interpersonal capacity and functioning. The subcomponents of the Interpersonal Scale include Empathy, Social Responsibility, and Interpersonal Relationship.

Overall, the Interpersonal scale results indicate social adeptness, the ability to understand others, and to interact and relate well with people. Sue is typically responsible and dependable, and Sue most typically functions well in tasks involving making contact with others and teamwork. Well developed interpersonal skills are also important for those involved in management and leadership.

Empathy Subscale Score (116):

The responses indicate an individual with a good awareness, understanding, and appreciation of the feelings of others. Sue probably will go out of her way to help others, and will try to avoid hurting other people's feelings.

Social Responsibility Subscale Score(111):

The reponses pertaining to the Social Responsibility scale indicate an individual who is cooperative and constructive. Sue is probably quite responsible and dependable and will do her best to help people.

Interpersonal Relationship Subscale Score(118):

The responses are indicative of an individual who has good interpersonal skills. Sue probably is able to establish and maintain mutually satisfying relationships that have the proper degree of intimacy. She is comfortable with the giving and receiving of affection.

ADAPTABILITY EQ SCALE SCORE(115):

This part of the EQ-i is composed of the Reality Testing, Flexibility, and Problem Solving Scales and examines how successful one is in coping with environmental demands based on one's ability to effectively size up and deal with problematic situations.

The Adaptability component is substantially higher than average. Sue is probably very flexible and able to adjust to changing circumstances and situations. The responses to the Adaptability component of the EQ-i suggest she is practical, realistic, and does not over-indulge in fantasy. She understands problematic situations and can usually come up with effective and solutions. Not only is this a valuable personal attribute for home and family life, but those with good adaptability thrive in work settings that require someone who is 'down to earth', clear thinking, and adapts easily to changing demands.

Reality Testing Subscale Score (118):

The results for this subscale indicate an individual who is able to evaluate the correspondence between what she experiences (the subjective) and what in reality exists (the objective). These people are often described as realistic, "well grounded" and "tuned in" to what's going on around them.

Flexibility Subscale Score (117):

The EQ-i results indicate an adequate ability to adjust emotions, thoughts, and behavior to changing situations and conditions. Sue usually finds it fairly easy to learn new things, doesn't become too fixed into routines, and remains open-minded to differing opinions and ways of thinking.

Problem Solving Subscale Score (100):

The responses to the Problem Solving scale indicate that Sue is moderately successful approach to solving problems. Improvement is possible, however, and may center around trying to take a more methodical approach, taking the time to consider alternative solutions and by carefully thinking through each step.

STRESS MANAGEMENT EQ SCALE SCORE (102):

The Stress Management component of the EQ-i consists of the Stress Tolerance and Impulse Control Subscales. One or both of the two subcomponents of stress management is low. This finding may indicate a tendency to nervousness or anxiety, and difficulties handling stressful situations. The descriptions of the subcomponents are given below.

Stress Tolerance Subscale Score (112):

Sue has good Stress Tolerance. Although the responses suggest some feelings of anxiety and nervousness from time to time, Sue is able to overcome these feelings and withstand adverse events and stressful situations. Sue is generally able to cope with stress actively and positively.

The results from my personality test in LA (2 of 3).

95

Impulse Control Subscale Score (92):

Sue's ability to resist or delay impulses, drives, and temptations to act is about comparable to others in the population. Like others, there are probably times when she feels impatient but this is not unusual and probably rarely results in overreacting or losing control.

GENERAL MOOD EQ SCALE SCORE (117):

The sub-components of this composite scale consist of the Optimism and Happiness subscales. These components of the EQ-i measure one's general feeling of contentment and overall outlook on life.

Both components of the General Mood scale are well developed, and descriptions of these components are given below.

Optimism Subscale Score (116):

Sue appears to be highly Optimistic. She is typically able to look at the brighter side of life and maintain a positive attitude, even in the face of adversity. This characteristic is usually helpful in handling difficult or stressful situations.

Happiness Subscale Score (115):

The responses to the items on this scale indicate a person who feels satisfied with her life, who enjoys the company of others, and who is able to derive a great deal of pleasure and fun from life. Sue probably has a happy disposition and is pleasant to be with.

PROFILE SUMMARY:

Overall, the EQ-i results indicate well developed emotional intelligence. However, there are fairly large differences in the scores for the 15 content scales indicating areas of relative strength and areas of improvement.

The three highest subscales are: Self-Regard (119), Emotional Self-Awareness (119), and Self-Actualization (118). The three lowest subscales are: Impulse Control (92), Problem Solving (100), and Social Responsibility (111).

SIMPLE STRATEGIES FOR DEVELOPMENT

Strategies for improving the areas that yielded the three lowest EQ-i scores:

Impulse Control:

Get into the habit of counting to 10 before acting. Learn the importance of listening to others.

Problem Solving:

Identify others with valuable opinions. Share problems with them. Ask for their advice. Involving other people in the process is often helpful. When working out problems, take the time to sit down and make a list of possible alternative solutions, and list the pros and cons of those solutions.

Social Responsibility:

Think of how the situation affects others. Is there something that can be done to help out? Is there a way to make a positive contribution?

CLOSING REMARK

This narrative report is meant as an aid to help understand the results of the BarOn EQ-i. Combined with other information, the EQ-i can help identify areas of strength to as well as areas that could be improved. It is hoped that this report adds some insight into the emotional and social functioning of the respondent by summarizing the responses given.

The results from my personality test in LA (3 of 3).

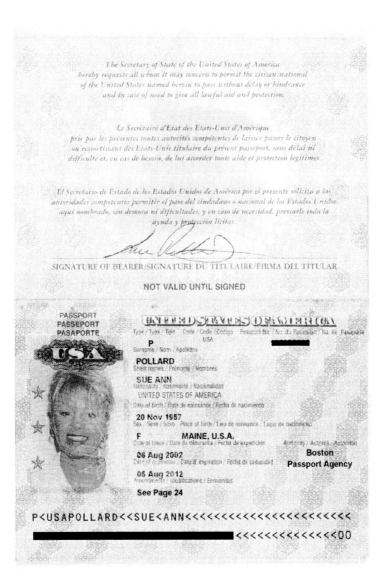

I want to know: Who *likes* their passport picture?

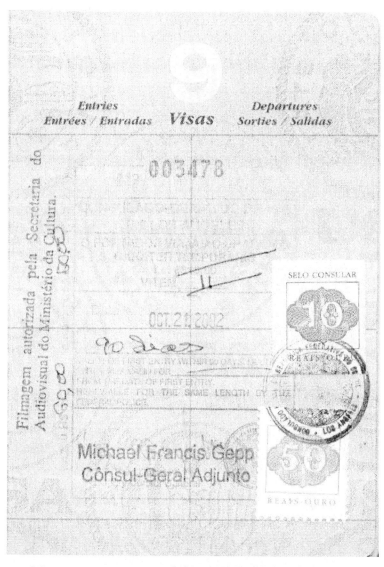

My passport stamped for Brazil, The Amazon!

The Alternate Survivor

Sue Pollard

From: ████████ com
Sent: Thursday, October 24, 2002 8.15 PM
To: ████████ com
Subject: No Subject

Got the results, thank you SO much for getting that done so quickly!

Keeping my fingers crossed for you ..

xoxo
Joc

Jocelyn Green
Contestant Coordinator
████████ office
████████ cell

11/1.2002

An email from Jocelyn confirming receipt of my
medical results at the very end.

Hand-written note of encouragement from Joceyln.

Five

Oh Brother!

A year and a half passed. It was now summer of 2004. And believe it or not I still thought about *Survivor* at least 3 to 4 times a day! You have to realize what type of person I am. As I said earlier: In my business I can walk into 10 new accounts and actually get eight or nine new customers—and most people would be happy with that. But not me: I dwell on that one customer I didn't get. I keep trying until I get them. It's just who I am.

Anyway, I was having one of the worst days of my life and for whatever reason I remember it as though it were just the other day. I was driving home on Chapel Road in Wells. I had been working a lot that week and was trying to keep a positive attitude even though it seemed like everything was going wrong that day: My help was slacking. The building I was renting was being sold and we had to move my Suzipoo business. I had just ordered 50,000 plastic bags for my candy to be packed in and they were the wrong bags (or at least they had made them incorrectly). I had to pick up my three children all at different locations but all at the same time. My son had a doctor's appointment for a sports' physical. And besides all of that, I was running late. I remember thinking, "Why can't life be a little easier sometimes?"

And right about then I looked at my cell phone and saw that I had a voice message. I pressed the buttons to listen and this is what I heard:

"Hi, Suzi! It's Lynne Spillman from *Survivor*. Call me! --- --- ----. I have another show I think you would be great on." I got home and Lynne Spillman had left a message on my home phone and my business phone, too! One of her messages (that I still have not erased!) says, "Hi Suzi! I have called you on all the phone numbers I have for you." "Please call me ASAP!" So I called.

"Hello."

"Hi Lynne. It's Sue Pollard."

"Sue! I'm so glad you called me back! I'm calling because I think you would be great for the upcoming *Big Brother* 5."

I said, "Oh, I thought you were calling me for *Survivor* . . ." I must admit that I was disappointed. As with *Survivor*, I had never watched *Big Brother* before my friend Richard had mentioned it to me, so I felt like 'H*ere we go again!*' But somehow it was different this time.

I remember saying to Lynne that I really had never watched *Big Brother*. But she had told me not to worry and that I'd be great for the part. She told me that she'd given my name to a Tedd Schermerhorn and that he would be calling me soon.

###

"You are just the perfect type for *Big Brother*. Don't you remember me telling you that when you were in L.A.? I asked you if you had ever watched *Big Brother* and I said you would be perfect because you're like the Barbie type."

I thought about it and I remember that she *had* seemed to be a big fan of *Big Brother*. I recall one night, in fact, when I was in LA as a finalist for *Survivor*. It was approaching eight o'clock and Lynne was rushing me back to my room because she didn't want to miss *Big Brother*. She kept telling me how much she loved the show. But instead of watching it myself I probably went back to my room and watched *The Perfect Storm* for the twenty-fifth time. Ha!

When I got off the phone with Lynne I remember thinking to myself: *Well, why did you people put me through what you did for Survivor if you didn't think I would make a good contestant?* But instead I thought about the fact that I had no other way to apply for *Survivor* again, so I just kept my thoughts to myself and went along with her.

###

I had about 18 hours to prepare for my adventure this time. Lynne had called me around two o'clock my time and, while I was waiting for a call from the casting director, I sent my girls to *Best Buy* to buy the DVD of the previous season of *Big Brother* (*Big Brother 4*). I told myself that this time I was at least going to know who the host was! My family and I watched the entire season of the show that night and we were not really impressed.

It seemed more appropriate for someone living a single person's lifestyle (which was *so* not me!). But I said w*hat the heck* and decided to give it a shot anyway. Again, I had felt that being on TV was a chance of a lifetime and that you never really knew if you didn't give something a try!

So even though it wasn't *Survivor*, I thought that I should at least check out what they might have to offer me. So I waited for the phone call from Tedd and, sure thing, he did call.

At about three-thirty the phone rang and I saw a California number on the Caller ID. I answered.

"Hi Sue! This is Tedd Schermerhorn—one of the casting directors from *Big Brother*. How are you?"

I said "Great!"

Then he asked me what I thought about coming out to LA on such short notice and having an interview for the show. I said with an upbeat attitude, "I'd love to." He asked me to fill out an application on-line and send it via overnight mail. I said I would but I would never have time to put a three minute VHS video together. He said, "Don't worry about it. But could you send in your *Survivor* audition tape?" I said, "I don't know if I am supposed to do that or not."

"Oh, don't worry: Lynne won't mind."

So I said I would fill it out and send it right in, overnight.

As Lynne and Martha had done before, Tedd explained the process to me. I was to pick up my e-ticket at the airport. And once again I was to take a taxi to the hotel where we would be staying. I felt like I was having déjà vu.

Pick up my e-ticket. Get a taxi to the hotel. Save the receipt. They would reimburse me.

That night I called my dear friend Sharma and told her what was going on. She loved *Big Brother* and she came over to my house and helped me fill out my application. It was quite long but we got it done and I had it in the mail by 4:30 the next day.

And so, in the whirlwind spirit of the whole Reality TV world, I uprooted myself again and *the next morning* I was on a plane bound for L.A.

This time the trip went quickly. I wasn't as anxious as before and I'd brought myself plenty of things to do and to read. Before I knew it the plane was about to land. The captain came over the intercom and said that we would be landing in 15 minutes in sunny Los Angeles, California. Touch down. Here I was again. In LA for a reality TV program.

As I watched the cab driver load my overstuffed bag into the trunk of the taxi I thought to myself *Here we go again!* It was just like the *Survivor* process.

And even though I wasn't as excited as I was for *Survivor*, I was still planning to give it my best. I got a taxi and gave the taxi driver the hotel address and we started off for the hotel. Again I found myself looking around. All the different stores and restaurants and the landscape was so different from what I am used to. I imagined one of the lobsterman from Damariscotta being here and I laughed to myself. It truly would seem like another planet to them!

We got to the hotel and I got a receipt again. Thirty-one dollars—just as it was when I tried out for *Survivor*! Weird! That must be the price of a taxi for all reality TV contestants. Ha! I got to the hotel and checked in. The room was ready for me under my name. I went up to the room and called them to say that I was there.

Whoever answered the phone asked me to come to a certain room. So I did. I knocked on the door and I heard a voice, "Come in!" There were three people in the room. Cameras and wires were everywhere, and a big camera for taking still pictures.

They made small-talk with me and asked me about my trip, how my flight was and then told me they needed to take a few pictures of me.

I was not feeling very good about things already. And I usually have pretty good intuition. I can't explain it, exactly. Maybe it was a sense of casual unprofessionalism from the staff, or a feeling of aimlessness to the whole process. It's not that the people weren't nice to me. They were perfectly nice—if a bit cavalier and closemouthed. It's just that everything seemed too *unplanned*. And it seemed as if nobody was telling me what I was supposed to do, and when I would be meeting with the producers of the show.

Anyway, the conversation was short and I was sent back to my room to hibernate. But this time I was a little smarter. I had brought my laptop, the

Big Brother 4 series on DVD, and lots of paperwork to keep me busy.

After about an hour had passed I got a call from a girl who asked me to meet her in the restaurant downstairs. So off I went, not even having a clue what this girl looked like, but hoping that she would be more informative.

When I got downstairs I looked around for a moment and finally saw a girl who was about 5 foot 4 with a long blond ponytail, waving at me. I walked over and she introduced herself.

Well here was at least one small advantage *Big Brother* had over *Survivor*: At least this time whenever we had meals one of the casting crew would sit with us! She began asking me about who I was, what was it like to be a finalist for *Survivor*? She asked me what my interests were and all kinds of questions that had nothing to do with *Big Brother* (or so I thought, anyway!).

So I started asking her questions about her job. She told me she worked on the set of *Charmed* and told me how it was to work with Alyssa Milano, Rose McGowan and Holly Marie Coombs. The whole time she was talking about the show *Charmed* and I was trying to act like I knew the cast from *Charmed* when I didn't even have a clue.

Then she started asking me more questions about my experience being a finalist on *Survivor*. And because of the secretive way that *Survivor* had been run I wondered if I should even be talking to her about my experience with *Survivor*? At this point I was confused. Here I was having been called just two days earlier by Lynne Spillman to see if I would be interested in being on *Big Brother* 5 and getting excited thinking she was calling me for *Survivor*. And now I was back to sitting in a very lonely hotel room struggling to figure out what was going on.

Our lunch together was short and was over before I knew it. She said it was great to meet me and that I could go back to my room now. So off I went to the elevator and back up to my room wondering what I had gotten myself into! Was anyone ever going to tell me what I was supposed to do?

I was back in my room. But on the way I had noticed a Coke machine in the hallway. So I grabbed some quarters, went to the peek hole in my door, and checked to see if anyone was out there. I didn't want to get into trouble! I cautiously opened the door and rushed out to get a diet Coke. While I was out I saw an ice machine so I said *"What the heck. I'm going to get some ice too!"* How messed up is it that they still had me questioning whether it was okay to buy myself a Coke! But the show was called *Big Brother*, after all!

I went back to my room and made a phone call to a family friend named Terri Powell. She knew the whole *Survivor* story.

"Hello Terri! It's Sue. You're not going to believe this but I'm in LA as a finalist for *Big Brother*!"

She busted out laughing.

"You hot ticket! Where did all of this come from?"

I proceeded to tell her the story and all she could say was "Leave it up to you! Sue, you never quit! One of these days you will make it for sure!"

We laughed for a while and then I hung up and called my husband. I told him what was happening.

"My room is nice. I have a very comfy queen-sized bed and a nice television—though not quite the same view I had for *Survivor*. I'll have to put some crumbs out on the window ledge to see if my pigeon friend is around!"

Believe it or not I actually did put some crackers out there but no pigeon ever came!

And then I hung up the phone and started to watch the *Big Brother* series over and over again. At least this time I would know that the host was Julie Chen. Another day went by and I got a call to meet a gentleman downstairs for lunch. I went down again not knowing who I was looking for, or what the meeting would involve.

As soon as I entered the room a man flagged me over like he was herding sheep and told me to come with him. He could have been a serial killer for all I knew but again, in the spirit of reality TV casting you are supposed to be a good little camper and do what they tell you to. You just have to let go of your skepticism and trust that there is an underlying purpose for everything they have you do. And so I went with him.

He was acting very weird, very fidgety, and on edge. It was almost as if he were on some kind of drugs. And if he wasn't, well then he just didn't seem right.

He also didn't talk much during dinner. And once I realized that he wasn't going to ask me any questions or tell me about what I was doing there, I realized that he was mostly going to remain silent. So I ended up doing almost all of the talking myself (which, of course, wouldn't surprise anyone who knows me!).

I wonder now if his silence was another test. Were they trying to see how I would react under different circumstances? Was I being videotaped while I tried to fill in the silence? It sure seems a fair bet to me that I was. But at the time I figured it was just all small-talk with crew members, and that at some point they were really going to *interview* me!

Anyway, I started asking him about his job, what he liked about it, and so on. And after a while I felt like I was interviewing him. He asked me to leave the table and sit in another chair across the room for a minute so he could think about something. Weird. But, when anyone in the crew asks you to do something, you just do it. So I did.

Right across from me was another guy who kept staring at me. And even when I looked right at him he wouldn't look the other way. That went on for about 15 minutes. I was so uncomfortable that I was squirming in my seat. When *Big Brother* 5 aired I would find out that he was one of the contestants. His name was Mike, the older guy on the show. He would be the first one who was voted off.

The next day, day two in my *Big Brother* LA experience, I got a phone call to meet downstairs to go over to CBS Studios. It was the same thing as it was with *Survivor*: a big white van with eight people in it. Now knowing some of them from the show I

115

can identify them as Holly, Jennifer, Mike, Natalie and Karen.

We all rode over together in silence. As before, we were not allowed to speak, although this time the girl driving the van actually talked to us. She asked if we would like a piece of gum, then passed around a big pack with enough for everyone in the back. She asked us to be sure that we didn't talk. And then she said, "You're all adults. You know the process." She seemed a lot easier going than the drill sergeant who was driving the van for *Survivor*.

We got to CBS and there I was walking through the same walkway into the exact same building and the exact same conference room as *Survivor*. We started out watching the same TV. Nothing in the room had changed except that this time when you walked in there was a picture of Jeff Probst on the left wall. Actually, now that I think about it, that picture might have been there the last time too, but I may have been too nervous and excited to have noticed it. And of course, I thought with a smile, I also didn't know who Jeff Probst was then. Ha!

Otherwise everything else seemed the same. We had to walk through the same security station. And I remembered the beautiful blue-cushioned chairs and a huge picture window that overlooked the highway and the entrance to the studio.

Once again, we were given a big speech.

"Some of you have already seen the producers and some of you have not. You may or may not be going in today, either. They may have already looked at your audition tape and decided that you're a shoe-in or you're not. If you're not asked to come and meet with them do not interpret it either way."

So I'm sitting there thinking to myself that I *had* to be having an interview because the only videotape they had of me was the one from *Survivor*. But an hour went by in the waiting room and suddenly it was time to go. I'm sure I looked rather dumbfounded that they hadn't asked to see me.

We all piled back into the van and off we went. I was looking around, not having a clue why I was even there and what was going on. And nobody seemed to care.

When we got back to the hotel we were told to go to our rooms and wait for the next phone call. The phone rang and I answered. I was asked to come downstairs and take a seat. But do not sit near anyone else. Or talk to anyone. So I headed down to the lobby.

I looked around and there were about twenty people sitting alone. I recognized a few from riding over in the bus. We all sat there just staring at each other and each one of us was probably thinking the same thing. Which one of us was going to make it?

Maybe it was the fact that I'd already been through something similar to this experience with *Survivor* or maybe it was just that my heart just wasn't into the whole *Big Brother* concept the way that it was *Survivor*. But I was probably the only one who wasn't *into it* like the others.

We sat there for a very long time and nothing happened. Then, all of a sudden, a girl entered the room and came directly over to me and said, "Okay Sue, you can go back to your room."

I said, "That's it? We were just asked to come down and sit here?"

"You're being watched. Everything you do. So they may have already made their decision."

"Who? Who are you talking about? And what could I have possibly done wrong? Snuck out to get a diet coke?"

By this time I think they could really hear the frustration in my voice. I was sent back to my room again and told that someone would be calling me.

It must have been obvious that I was getting frustrated. They must have been watching me on a hidden camera and seeing me fidget. And maybe somehow they could tell that my heart wasn't in it.

Five or Six hours passed. Nothing. So I called the number I was given and asked to speak to Tedd. He wasn't around. I asked if she could have him call me. Whoever had answered the phone asked me if there was anything she could help me with?

I proceeded to tell her that I was confused about this whole process and she asked me why.

I said, "First of all, I have not had any type of interview like I did for the *Survivor* process. And I feel like I don't even know what I'm doing here!"

I felt that I had been called out to California because they wanted me on the show. And I had *assumed* that since I hadn't even applied for the show that someone out here would have at least met with me when I'd arrived and talked with me. Instead I had been left in the dark and treated strangely.

She said, "I will have Tedd call you."

I said "Thank you."

About forty-five minutes went by and the phone rang.

"Hi Sue, it's Tedd. Someone told me you're confused about the process?"

I was really frustrated and not at my best. And I took it out on Tedd. I said "What process? You call this a process?"

And then it occurred to me to ask him, "Did you ever receive my application and my video from *Survivor* that you asked me to send you?"

He acted like he didn't know what I was talking about. He seemed distracted. Then he said, "Oh yeah, I think we got it."

To myself I was screaming inside '*WHAT? I think we got it? Does anyone here have their act together or what?*'

I'm telling you the whole experience was strange. It was like I was being subjected to the casting equivalent of method acting. I mean, was the *entire* Big Brother casting experience based on watching you via hidden cameras? Was there *any* of the formal interviewing that I'd done with *Survivor* for this show?

Reflecting on the whole thing I think that that is exactly what my Big Brother experience was all about. But even if I had known that then, and really understood it, I'm not sure I could have acted any differently. Deep down inside, I wanted to go on *Survivor* and nothing else was going to make me happy.

Tedd apologized and said "Thank you so much for coming out here on such short notice. We will be in touch." And then he proceeded to give me my itinerary for my flight back to Maine in the morning.

I hung up the phone and felt even more confused. I called my husband to tell him what had happened.

He could tell that I was upset and reminded me that I would be home the next day and that I could tell him all about it then.

"I love you."

"I love you too, Honey."

I watched TV for a while and then before I knew it I must have fallen asleep because my alarm was going off and I was in the shower getting ready to leave the hotel. I walked down to the lobby and didn't see anyone I recognized. I asked the front desk to call for a taxi. I was feeling very low and confused.

I remember looking around at the hotel and thinking that I couldn't wait to get home to people who acted normal. At the time I didn't consider that I was probably on camera the entire time—in my room, while I was on the phone, in the hallway—everywhere. And it didn't occur to me that they were probably trying to put me in uncomfortable positions on purpose, like I was in some giant laboratory experiment.

But who knows what they were looking for? To this day, I'm not sure what it was that the other candidates for the show did to earn their way onto *Big Brother*. Did they snap, too, but in more entertaining ways than I did? Did they not snap at all and thereby prove their patience and willingness to be cooped up for three months while every aspect of their life was being filmed?

But at the time none of these things had crossed my mind and all I could think about was that the whole process had seemed aimless and unorganized and no one had told me in advance how the process was supposed to work. And I was disappointed in myself for letting them keeping me in the dark.

I got in the taxi and headed toward the airport.

I called Tedd when I got home the next day. I asked him what had just happened and why they had even had me come out to L.A. His response was that they had just wanted to meet me. I could tell that he was going out of his way to be nice. He must have thanked me two or three times saying "Sue, thank you so much for taking your time to come out to L.A. It was great to meet you!" And so on. He also told me that they would be in touch, to let me know if I had been selected.

It was all very strange and the whole thing was so disappointing. I mean, when I'd gotten on the plane for Big Brother I had really thought that someone was going to meet me when I got out there and, I don't know, maybe talk to me about the show? Especially since I hadn't even applied and they had called *me*! But they had just treated me like any other applicant. That's fine, I suppose, in the spirit of fairness. But at least someone could have told me that before I was subjected to another round of psychological torture. It just didn't seem right.

That said, and to tell you the truth, I just don't personally think that *Big Brother* is as compelling as *Survivor*, and it's definitely not my style. Plus, I would have had to be away from my family for three months, rather than forty days, and that was just too long for me! But, always being optimistic and willing to take chances, I had thought, *Oh well— nothing ventured, nothing gained.*

But, in the end, it was such a different experience than the process of *Survivor*. I mean even with all of the alone time, my eleven days for *Survivor* were awesome compared with *this*.

I loved the tests and the interactions. And things actually *happened* during my eleven days with *Survivor*. I'd gotten six shots. They had stamped my passport to go to some wild island. And the excitement had been unbelievable.

But for me, the *Big Brother* process seemed so unprofessional and dehumanizing by comparison. From the beginning, the whole thing had felt awkward and uncomfortable and seemed like a waste of *my* time and energy and a waste of the *studio's* money.

When all is said and done I will say that—and no sour grapes here, really—I am very grateful that I never made it on *Big Brother*. Because if the casting process was any indication of how the whole show would have been I would have been miserable. I'll take a deserted island with no water, sleep or food any day. Just give me some competition!

Despite my disappointment and frustration, to this day I truly believe that my *Big Brother* experience was part of some greater plan. And it *does* makes me wonder, that of all the thousands of applications they get, why would they ever called someone as a finalist that hadn't even applied.

The answer, it seems pretty clear to me, is that they saw something in me.

Lynne Spillman had said to me: "Sue, you probably will make it. They are down to the finalists and you would be great on this show."

So did they ever call me back to ask me to be on *Big Brother* 5? Or let me know that I *wasn't* selected? Well, once again, I was told that they would call me and they never did.

Whatever happened to common courtesy? A phone call to let someone know that they didn't make it—after all of the effort that these candidates are putting into the process—is a simple thing that would go a long way. I hope that I am the exception. And I hope that, in most cases, when someone from CBS tells a potential candidate for a reality TV series that they will call them back, that they actually do call them back.

For that matter, had someone met with me—even briefly—when I'd arrived in California for *Big Brother*, the whole end-result might have been different, too. Had someone talked to me and told me that they were going to inject me into the process—just as if I were any of the other candidates—I would at least have known what to expect. But they hadn't.

My advice to the casting folks on these reality shows? Try to remember that your candidates are human beings and not emotionless commodities.

Sue Pollard: 0/2
Reality TV Shows: 0/2

Six

The Not-so-Amazing Casting Call

Even the *Big Brother* experience wasn't enough to stop me from trying. And I still felt passionate about being on a reality show after making it as far as I did with *Survivor*.

In fact, after Big Brother I actually got the bug back worse than I had it before. Was it seeing Lynne's number on my Caller ID? Was it my amazement that I'd been called to interview for a show I hadn't even applied for? Well, whatever it was, it gave me renewed confidence that people saw something in me that they thought would make good television.

But were there any other shows out there that were as good as Survivor?

So many people had asked me why I hadn't tried out for *The Amazing Race*. I used to say that I really hadn't watched the show.

But one of my good friends, Sharma—who helped me with my last minute Big Brother application—wouldn't stop bringing it up!

"Sue, give it a try! I have a bunch of VHS tapes from the past season of *The Amazing Race*. Come on over tonight and let's watch them and we'll see what you think. You would do such a good job on *The Amazing Race*, I'm telling you!"

I said, "Well I've heard that before!" And I laughed.

She said, "We've got to get you on a reality show because you're such a piece of work and I think you would be such a great entertainer."

So I said "Okay, thanks for pumping me up! Let's go and watch *The Amazing Race!*"

So we went to her house and watched *The Amazing Race.* I thought the show was rather interesting. It wasn't as good as *Survivor* but hey: Why not give it a try?

So, believe it or not, here we went again . . .

You will probably think I am crazy but I really was excited to try out for *The Amazing Race.* And the *Big Brother* experience really hadn't soured me at all. Big Brother just wasn't my style. I'm a girl of action and competition—not psychological tension and drama!

But now I had to find a partner to do this race with. And one person quickly came to mind. I have known him all of my life. We used to ride dirt bikes together as kids. He's extremely competitive and a great guy. Please allow me to introduce you to Bobby Winn.

Bobby is an avid runner and sixteen-time marathon winner. He is known all over the state of Maine and even has gone abroad to race. He has won over two-hundred and seventy-seven road races! And when he runs he makes it look like it's fun! I approached him and asked him if he would consider doing *The Amazing Race* with me? His response was to laugh.

I said, "Bobby, I'm serious".

"Oh, I have no doubt you are."

Ha! Wise-guy! And that's why I love him!

But I said, "So what do you think?"

He gave my favorite answer, "I've never even watched the show."

And then he followed up with, "Is that the one they eat gross stuff on?"

"No! That's Fear Factor!"

So I told him what the show was about. He listened to me, but he was pretty skeptical and told me he'd have to think about it.

The next day I went into school and I talked with a friend of mine, a teacher who happens to watch every reality show that there is.

I say, "Hey Donny, I'm considering doing *The Amazing Race* with Bobby Winn. What do you think?"

His response was "Oh my God you two would be perfect for *The Amazing Race!*"

Well of course that was just the answer I was looking for.

So the next day I went to the house that Bobby was building in Ogunquit and I trudged right in, like I often did, and asked again.

"So Bobby, are you going to do this with me or what?"

He smiled and said, "You'll kill me!"

I laughed and smiled back, "Only if we lose!"

But then he said the words I was hoping to hear, "Lets do it, Sue."

I was psyched!

Now of course I am a pro at making reality audition tapes and filling out the applications at this point. So I said, "O.K. this is what we need to do. We've got to get together this week because the deadline for the application is July 26th. And today is July 15th."

So Bobby and I got together with my dear friend Sharma Damren who was an *Amazing Race* fan in addition to *Big Brother*. She's a piece of work and I love her. She's outgoing and has a great attitude.

I arranged for all of us to meet at Sharma's house on July 17th. That didn't give us much time to get this done but I knew we could do it.

Two days later we all met at Sharma's house as planned, to start filling out the applications. We had quite a few laughs with the comments we made to one another. You know the type—the typical good-natured harassment you reserve for your friends. At one point, Sharma came up with a good one that ended up sticking with us during the rest of the video-making process—and even made it into the video itself!

Sharma suddenly became very serious and said to Bobby,

"You know Bobby, that Sue will kill you if you two don't win this"

And, of course, I couldn't help but pipe in with my two cents. "Bobby already knows that. Isn't that right, Bobby?"

Bobby just laughed.

After filling out the application I said, "Okay, now we need to do a three-minute video. How about this Saturday? I will come up to the house you're building with my tool belt on and we can pretend I helped you build the house. What do you think?"

They both liked the idea (or at least bowed to my vast experience) and we booked it.

So Saturday came and I got there just as I said—at nine o'clock sharp, with Sharma along to videotape us. We started off having Bobby and I standing inside the unfinished house with our tool belts on.

My tool belt, of course, had never been used and Bobby's tool belt had been used so much it was as soft as a pair of gloves! Sharma started shooting and I swung my hammer down as if I knew what I was doing. Of course I really had no clue, and I dropped it right on my freaking foot! So before I could even get the first words out that we had been practicing, I had to yell "CUT!"

Well, Sharma and Bobby literally collapsed to the floor laughing. Not only did I not know how to swing a hammer, but I obviously didn't even know how to *hold* a hammer. After they were done laughing at me (and it took several minutes, let me tell you!), I said, "Okay, I'm done amusing you two so let's get this damn video done!"

Eventually they did stop laughing and we got back to work. Bobby and I were standing on the stairs in the middle of his unfinished house. I'm sure it's hard to believe but *I* was planning to do most of the talking! Sharma gave us the thumbs up—that was my queue.

I started the video by saying,

"Hey, *Amazing Race*! I heard you were looking for two amazing people? Well look no further because you've found them!

"I would like to introduce you to my dear friend of over 40 years: Bobby Winn. We've been friends all of our lives. We're competitive, driven and most of all, relentless. "

With that said I asked Bobby a question, "How do you feel about being stuck with me for two months?"

He looks at me and says,

"Let's stop talking about it already and do it!"

And although that's not what we had "scripted" for him to say, it was just the kind of thing I would have expected him to say under normal circumstances. He'd gotten me good and we both started laughing because I am such a camera hog and Bobby is very humble. Of course I had barely let him get a word in edge-wise! We couldn't get ourselves under control and for about the tenth time I had to yell "CUT!" while still laughing hysterically.

We started up again and walked out of the house. While Sharma filmed, I was talking for both of us and saying how great it would be to be on *The Amazing Race*.

"During the summer time when I'm not doing a million things, and Bobby isn't doing two million things, we built this new house together."

Sharma got a shot of the house that Bobby had been building for the last year. Then I continued,

"But in the fall we're going to have some free time and we want to do *The Amazing Race*."

For the next segment of the video we submitted, I had gone to a friend of mine who is a professional photographer. With his help, we put together a video from various news clips of Bobby winning numerous races.

There were a few clips from a Channel 6 News telecast of a Maine marathon race. One in particular was very special for Bobby. A year earlier, his best friend and running partner had been killed while riding his bike home from work. Bobby wanted to win this race more than any other because he and his partner had been training for this very marathon together. And, as if that weren't enough, Bobby had decided that he wanted to win the trophy for his friend's three-year-old daughter.

As Bobby crossed the finish line, winning in record time, the Channel 6 News reporter said, "Winn did just that: he wins in record-breaking time!"

The newscast went on to tell the story about Bobby's friend. And there wasn't a dry eye anywhere as Bobby took the little, three-year old girl from her mother's arms and held her in one arm and the trophy in the other. Tears were running down Bobby's cheeks. And you could tell that the race had not only been a physical and mental victory for him but also an emotional one. There was no way anyone else had a chance that day.

This man is Amazing. My friend, my choice, my partner for *The Amazing Race:* Bobby Winn. I'm sure you would agree that I made a great choice!

Besides all of Bobby's outstanding achievements, I also included some clips of my own:

my closing remarks (as Chair of the school board) at the opening of the school year, a brief clip of me with my husband and my children, me taking off on a motorcycle, and the Superintendent introducing me at a School Committee meeting.

His introduction went like this: "Now may I introduce to you the most energetic School Committee Chair in the United States, Sue Pollard. (The video showed all of the teachers with big smiles and clapping.)

For the one minute segment that was just for me, I put together a whole bunch of pictures of me and had the song *Instant Replay* playing in the background. It was really cool.

During Bobby's minute we showed him finishing first in a handful of races and there were news stations doing the narrative in the background. "Winn wins another marathon!" "Winn is first over the finish line!"

Then it showed Bobby talking to an actual cameraman, giving some great advice. It went like this:

"Running is a big part of my life. My philosophy is that the brave may not live forever but the cautious do not live at all! From now on, travel the road to who you think you are and whom you think you can be!"

My comment?

"Rock On, Bobby!"

Bobby went on to talk about how he had been to the *Nationals* and traveled all over the world running, how he had run in world championship races, and how awesome the whole experience had been.

Finally, the video showed Bobby and me together again, outside. I had my tool belt on again and I said,

"The bottom line, Amazing Race, is that if, after watching a minute of Bobby and a minute of me, you don't choose us, then you're obviously looking for a bunch of duds! And Babe, that's not either one of us! We're going to win this race; we don't even need to sleep.

"And actually, that was a question we had . . . *Can we run right through the night to get ahead?"*

We ended the tape right after that, with Bobby and me standing side by side.

Our video was done! Our applications were complete! I checked them over for the hundredth time to make sure I had everything in order. I packed the very professional and well-organized binder in an overnight Fed-Ex box and sealed it up. But somehow I still felt like something was missing.

I looked at the instructions on-line one last time, just to make sure that we had everything. Because I was afraid that if the application was not complete they would just throw it in the garbage. And then it came to me: I didn't put a copy of our passports in!

My first thought was *'Oh, my gosh! I hope Bobby has a passport!'* I flew down to his house and, thank God, he was there. I ran inside.

"Bobby, do you have a passport?"

Very calmly he says, "Yeah, why?"

"Because I need to put a copy of our passports in the package!"

No problem. Mr. Calm, Cool and Collected gave it to me and I bolted out of his house, ran down to the store to make a photocopy, looked through the package one last time and then sprinted into the post office. And he was supposed to be the runner of our pairing!

I had made about ten stickers for the outside of the Fed-Ex box with Amazing Race logos and pictures of Bobby and me all over the place. Before mailing it off I made a duplicate copy of everything just as I did for *Big Brother* and of course *Survivor*. I don't know why I did it exactly, but I thought it might come in handy one day. Of course I never dreamed at the time that this book was even going to happen!

I mailed the package on July 26, 2005—the very last day we could postmark it for the try-outs. Of course I had all of the tracking info and I went on-line the next day. Bingo! *Your package was received at 11:18 A.M. by World Race production of*

Marina del Ray, CA. Perfect! Now once again the waiting game began.

But I was confident (go figure!). I mean, the video was so awesome. And I'm not just saying that. *The Amazing Race* must have thought so too—since they called me two days after they received it!

On July 29th, 2005 at about 2:45 in the afternoon the phone rang.

I answered the phone without noticing the number on Caller ID.

"Hello?"

"Yes, may I speak with Sue Pollard?"

"Speaking."

"Hi Sue. This is Dana from *The Amazing Race.*"

I froze. Then I immediately put down whatever I was doing. I couldn't believe I was getting this call —and so quickly!

My daughter Miranda was in the kitchen with me when I answered the phone. She hadn't noticed my reaction yet and I tried to get her attention. I was waving my arms like crazy. Finally she noticed and she mouthed a question to me, "*Who is it?*"

I mouthed back to her, "*It's The Amazing Race*"! I could feel myself getting flustered. I don't know whether it was because *The Amazing Race* was calling me or just because I couldn't believe I was getting called from another reality TV show. But anyway, the conversation went like this:

"Hi Sue, my name is Dana Tomsic and I am one of the casting directors for *The Amazing Race*. We received your video and application and loved your energy but we were wondering why you didn't apply with your husband?"

I hadn't even really thought about it. It just hadn't occurred to me to consider Bob as a partner for the show. Don't get me wrong: my husband is a stud. And he'd do great on any of these shows. In fact, the more I thought about it, he would probably make for good TV too since he's such a good looking guy! But what would my children do if we were both gone for so long? I'm not sure how long I paused but I finally answered.

"I don't know, I guess the main reason is that I didn't want to leave our family with no parents for two months. And, of course, one of us would have to keep working to be able to support the whole family.

"I also had tried to think about who I knew that was in great physical shape and my friend Bobby came to mind."

She then asked me if I would consider redoing another tape and application with my husband.

I was immediately worried that Bobby would be offended if I just turned my back on doing the show with him. "What's the problem with doing the show with a friend? I know that other people do it all the time?"

"Well, we saw that short clip of your husband and your kids and we felt that you and your husband might have the type of chemistry we're looking for that we couldn't get from you and a friend. So, what do you think? Would you just make a video with you and your husband?"

I felt like I had nowhere else to take the conversation. She didn't seem to be leaving me any room. So I caved.

"Sure. I guess so". And then I made what was probably my fatal mistake of *this* reality TV show experience for me. And I kept talking.

"I can't believe that out of all the applications you received, *I* would get this call!"

"Why would you say that?"

I told her about being basically the next to go on *Survivor*, and just missing the cut by one.

And after that her voice changed.

"You were a finalist in California for *Survivor*?"

Never bashful of my accomplishments, I couldn't leave it at that.

"Not only a finalist but I also had all the shots, and my passport was stamped for Brazil, The Amazon."

"That's really weird. Lynne (meaning Lynne Spillman) didn't say anything to me about you and *Survivor*?"

Her tone had *definitely* changed. And I felt like I had lost her. Are you kidding me? What was it now? Some other freaky unwritten "rule" that couldn't be broken about finalists applying for another show?

But, as if Dana hadn't quite made up her mind yet, she kept talking.

"Well, anyway, will you still send in a video with you and your husband?"

"Sure, I'll get it done and I'll send it to you Monday."

"Great. I look forward to receiving it and I will give you a call either way."

She then proceeded to give me a different address so that my new tape would be sent directly to her.

"Dana, I will get this right out to you."

"Thanks again, Sue. Talk to you soon. Bye-bye."

I hung up the phone and looked at my daughter.

"Miranda, can you believe it? That was Dana from *The Amazing Race*! She wants me to send in a video with Dad!"

Taking after her mother, Miranda is a girl of action. "Well let's go find him!"

He was landscaping at a house about a mile from where we live.

I got out of the car and walked over to him and said, "You are *not* going to believe this! *The Amazing Race* just called!"

I remember my husband saying how crazy it was that I had been called three times when tens of thousands of people apply for these shows.

"It can't be just coincidental that they keep choosing you for these shows. You obviously have something they like."

Then I told him the catch . . .

"They want me to put a video together with *you*. It's not that they didn't like Bobby, but they thought I had the charisma and the energy they were looking for and they saw you in that short clip and they said they were looking for the husband & wife dynamic more than the Sue & friend dynamic.

"So, anyway, they want me to send in a video with you. What do you think?"

At first he looked up in the air and put his hand to his forehead. I really don't think he even knew what to say!

And being the ever-so patient person that I am, I asked him again.

"*Well*, what do you think?"

God love him. When he finally answered me he said, "Why not!"

In the meantime, I couldn't help but feel like I was betraying Bobby. He was so good about doing this with me! And it's something he probably wouldn't have ever done on his own. But I also know that Bobby knew this was a dream of *mine*, not his, and that he would be happy for me.

So my husband Bob came home from work with me, showered up, and we made our video in fifteen minutes. Just the bare basics. Nothing fancy like my prior videos, but it was cute and showed us together.

This is what we did. The video showed my husband coming in the front door, saying:

"I'm so pissed! My wife wants to go on *The Amazing Race* without me! She's going to be gone for two months! I have to be responsible for all three kids, the house, the bills and everything while she's out having fun with her friend Bobby!

"Well to heck with that! If she's going anywhere for two months it's going to be with me."

And it showed him sweeping me off the floor in his arms and walking out the door.

I thought it was great!

We called it a wrap and Bob filled out an application. We got everything all together and I once again put the whole thing in a Fed-Ex overnight box and shipped it off.

I checked the tracking info the next day and . . . Bingo! It was received the next day at the special address that Dana had given me.

So my husband and I waited—thinking that we would hear from her at anytime now. There probably wasn't an hour that would go by that I didn't think about her calling. I took my cell phone with me everywhere I went and I just waited.

I was feeling good that she had called in the first place. But, stupid me, I had believed her (like I did everyone else associated with reality TV!) when she told me that she would call me back. See the problem? I keep my word and I always expect the same from others. But unfortunately, it doesn't always work that way, does it?

A week went by and I heard nothing. But since—little did *they* know—I had kept Lynne's phone number, I called Dana back. I got her extension only because of my persistence. She answered.

"Hello, this is Dana."

"Hi Dana, this is Sue Pollard. I haven't heard back and you said you would call."

"Are you the one that just missed the cut on *Survivor* and was sent to do *Big Brother*?"

"Yes."

"Oh, I'm sorry Sue, but the producers turned you down for *The Amazing Race*."

I couldn't believe it. Were they upset with me because of how I reacted during the Big Brother "interview"? Was there some unwritten rule, as I mentioned earlier, that kept me from even being considered? What was the problem?

But out loud I said, "What? I can't believe this. I can't take another rejection!"

Dana replied with a tone of practical efficiency that made me vaguely recall Martha, back in Boston, "I know Sue. I hear that all the time from people." She *so* wanted me off the phone. She might as well have actually yelled the word "Next!" out loud into the phone!

And then she said to me, and these are her exact words, "Suzi, you have to just let it go."

Well now I was angry! Let it go? My dream? I don't think so! Not now. Not after everything I've been through!

It was all I could do to control myself and not vent my frustrations over the whole three-show experience on this woman!

I mean, come on! Making it to first alternate for *Survivor* was one thing. And being called up and flown out to do *Big Brother* one more thing. But then, out of thousands and thousands of videos, and without having even spoken to Lynne Spillman about me—or anyone else, apparently, Dana saw something in me that she thought would be great for reality television. So what's the problem, people?

What is *that*? Was the world of reality TV plotting against me, or what?

I was definitely feeling punchy. And I thought of so many flip things to say to Dana right then. *Maybe I should apply for America's top model now, then?* Oh no, I'm just a little too old for that one. *Oh I know! How about American Idol?* Oh, that's right: I'm over 28 and I don't sing! *The Apprentice, maybe—since I'm already an entrepreneur?* No, I wouldn't apply for the Apprentice until Donald does something with his hairdo!

Wait a minute! N*ow I've got it! I know the perfect show I should apply for: The Biggest Loser!* Ha!

Anyway, back to Dana. When I asked her what had made her call me in the first place, she had said, "We loved your energy! And you're so charismatic and fun we thought you'd be great!"

Well you know what, Dana? You're right about all of that. But don't tell me to let it go and to put this whole experience behind me! It's just not happening! Sorry, but it's impossible for me to let go of my dream! Just like I told you before, Mark Burnett, and Lynne Spillman: I will see you all out in LA!

And actually, Mark, I'm only taking your great advice: "Never, ever, give up!"

Seven

The Lessons I have learned

I learned a lot about myself from the experiences I've described in this book. One of the many positive things that came out of all of this is that it gave me the opportunity to reflect upon the things that I feel strongly about, and the things that make me who I am.

To be clear, I'm not saying that the casting experience for various reality TV shows inspired me to live my life like Gandhi. These principles were all with me long before my friend Richard talked to me about *Survivor* that day in my restaurant. But the act of writing this book—which never would have happened without my *Survivor* experience, of course—became an opportunity to look back over my life and reflect on the things that I feel are most important.

As a result of this introspection, I came up with, or clarified for myself really, seven guiding principles that define me. They are powerful because they are simple. And because they are so simple, they are truly something that could benefit anyone.

I would even be so bold as to suggest that if everyone in this country tried earnestly to live by these rules, then I think we could get back those feelings that we all felt (all too briefly) after 9/11. These are the core values of family and community, of Mom and apple pie. And they are also key ingredients to personal strength and independence.

Okay, so you get it by now: I refuse to quit and even more so I refuse to listen to the word *no*. But it goes deeper than that, because I believe that perseverance creates character. And character is at the heart of all seven of my driving principles.

My guiding principles are:

1. Remember that all things are possible if you don't give up.
2. Don't let yourself believe that anything is beneath you.
3. Every day is a gift and it needs to be opened.
4. Treat people the way that you want to be treated yourself.
5. Don't rely on others for your happiness or you'll too often be disappointed.
6. Always keep family a priority.
7. Always "ROCK ON!"

One: Remember that all things are possible if you don't give up.

You've heard this one before, but I truly believe it: My success started when I stopped being afraid to fail.

When I was young, every time I would fail at something and I would try it again I realized that I did better the second time. I learned it in small lessons, one at a time. But eventually, and often after repeated attempts, I would come to understand that I was reaching a point where I wasn't just getting better, but I was actually getting it *right*. From there, it was a short path to come to the decision that doing it *right* was the only way to do it. And that's when I knew that I would be successful. Now don't get me wrong: I don't get some sick pleasure from failure, and from doing things over and over again. But I'm intelligent enough to know when something just isn't right, and that I need to do it again.

It's not that I seek perfection, really. Okay, I *do* seek it but I also recognize that I can't ever have everything perfect. But I do know that at some point during the course of my trials I find myself looking at what I've done and I discover that I'm satisfied.

I also believe that, in order to reach that point—where I'm satisfied—the standards that I apply to my own work need to be higher than the standards of any outsider.

A very important truth in life (and one that too many people nowadays seem to have forgotten) is that nothing good comes easy. Even people who feel they are entitled to a good life eventually figure out that a good life isn't going to come and find them. But what separates the winners and the successful from the masses are drive, courage, and persistence.

You have to be willing to work long, hard hours and put in a lot of sleepless nights. And the day that you step out of your comfort zone is probably the day you will find yourself on the road to success. I truly believe that if I keep trying I will make it! So what if I fall a few times? It's how many times I get back up that matters. Just like I told Mark Burnett and all of the other producers during one of my interviews: I may fall down seven times but you can count on me getting back up eight! (And to those closet math geniuses who might be reading this book: no, I don't care that that doesn't make sense mathematically! Ha!)

I realize that this entire book itself is a lesson on not giving up, but I wanted to cover another example. I wanted to talk about how I got my product into L.L. Bean.

Getting into L.L.Bean seemed impossible to me for many months. I must have called them nine times (at least!) to try to get an appointment before I finally found the right buyer for my product.

Each time I called I would always get the same answer:

"No, thank you. We aren't interested because we already have a product that is very similar to yours."

Well I knew that they didn't really have a product even close to mine. But I'm also wise enough to know that it wasn't anything personal. They are a huge company and people are always trying to get L.L.Bean to sell their products. So the buyers there are justifiably leery of cold calls.

So one day I said, "Darn it, I'm going to make a huge basket with all of my products in it and deliver it to L.L.Bean myself!" And I did. I put in my *Maine Moose, Lobster*, and *Portland Head Lighthouse* cookie mixes that all have matching cookie cutters tied to the front.

I put in all of my doggy treats. And of course I made a fresh batch of *Moose Poo Kookies* for them to try! Then I drove up to Freeport and walked into security with an enormous basket. I introduced my company as Suzipoo and the first thing he asked was, "Are you *the* Suzipoo?" Apparently I had already established a reputation for persistence!

I smiled and said, "The one and only!"

He smiled back genuinely, took the basket, and promised to make sure the buyer, Patti, would get it. Well that was around 10:00 A.M. At 3:15 P.M. the same day my phone rang. I looked at the Caller ID and it read L.L.Bean. My heart skipped a beat and I had to take a deep breath before picking up the receiver.

"Hello, this is Suzipoo. How may I help you?" The person calling me said, "Hi Suzi, this is Patti from L.L.Bean. We love your product. Let's get together!"

And the rest is history! I have been doing a substantial amount of business with L.L.Bean ever since! I would also like to say that they treat me *extremely* well. I recall when I first started that I was sent a huge packet of information that they needed me to fill out. They needed me to comply with their EDI and ASN standards and their LMNOP! It was crazy! When I got the package I thought about how, if I were a quitter, that would have been a good time to quit.

But not this girl! I called them up and spoke to a wonderful woman named Lori who helped to make sure that everything I did was in compliance with their business processes and standards. She has been so awesome to me and has the patience of a saint! She wants to make sure I do everything right. And that is the only way to deal with a company like L.L.Bean. Their company stands for perfection and they expect anyone who deals with them to be the same way. Works for me!

After about, oh, I would say my fourth order, I was able to do it all myself and our business relationship has been great ever since. But my point is that every step of the process required hard work. Just convincing them to carry my product was hard. But it was only the beginning. Then I had to adapt myself to their systems. And I'll always have to deliver a quality product and provide them with quality service. And if I should ever slip? Then I have nobody to blame but myself if they sever our relationship. That's exactly as it should be.

So what's the lesson here? If I had listened to the word *no* then I guarantee you that I would not be in L.L.Bean today! And if I had balked at the hard work required to even do business with them once they were interested? Then my product would still not be carried by L.L.Bean just as plainly as if they'd never heard my name. Oh, wait a minute, my fax is ringing. Looks like it's three more orders from L.L.Bean! Nice talking to you, but I have to get to work!

Two: Don't let yourself believe that anything is beneath you.

I try to teach my own children, and the other children of our community, that they should never look down on anyone else, or consider something beneath them.

For me, it's not even so much that I feel that nothing is beneath me as it is that I see the good in people, look beyond their weaknesses, and just respect those around me, in general. I also find value and satisfaction in doing many things that others don't. For example, how could I feel that sweeping the floor is beneath me? Somebody has to do it, right? And if it has to get done, and there's nobody else around to do it, then I roll up my sleeves and I do it. I can't even understand how somebody could feel that they are too good to sweep the floor. That's just arrogance, in my opinion—and it's unhealthy.

There's confident. There's cocky. And there's arrogant. I'll be the first to admit that I'm extremely confident, and maybe a little cocky. And some people might feel that I cross the line into arrogance. They're entitled to their opinion.

But in my mind, one of the key differences between positive self-confidence and all of the negative implications of arrogance is whether you think of your own worth in terms of your own personal standards and goals or whether you think of them only in comparison with others around you.

I was once asked if I thought I was better than other people. My response was immediate.

"No, not at all. But there is no one out there better than me, either."

I recognize that we're all different and we all have our individual strengths and weaknesses. But that doesn't mean that any one of us is better than anybody else.

Arrogant people, on the other hand, *do* believe that they are better than others and that they are "above" doing certain things. In my opinion, arrogant people must have very low self-confidence and are probably trying to boost their own sense of self by comparing themselves with those around them. Any time they can point to someone else's weaknesses they can pat themselves on the back for being better in those areas themselves.

"Oh, look at her: she's got no self-control!"

"Do you believe that they would be caught driving around in that car?"

"Get out of my way. Can't you see that I'm trying to get to my seat?"

"Ha-ha! He can only bench 150 pounds!"

Arrogant people make judgments about others even as they are propping themselves up.

"I have willpower. You're fat."

"I drive a Mercedes. You're poor."

"I'm an important person. You don't matter."

"I'm physically strong. You're weak."

Arrogant people seem to believe that there are things, activities, and people who are beneath them. This attitude creates negativity in the world. It deteriorates community. And it creates divisions between people. An arrogant parent will unconsciously teach their children by example that there are things in the world that are beneath them. And the negativity is perpetuated. At a cocktail party with their "friends" (though I doubt they even have any *true* friends) they risk infecting those around them with arrogance by their words and actions. Cliques form. Negativity spreads.

But, even as strongly as I feel about arrogance (I hate it! Who doesn't?). I feel even more strongly that self-confidence, and even a certain amount of cockiness, can be a healthy way to approach life. Because I think that self worth and self-confidence are so important for everyone in the world.

If there is one thing that I try to teach every child who I come in contact with, it's that they can literally do anything that they set their mind to. Is that an arrogant thing to say, or think? I don't think so. On the contrary, I believe it's the key to a person's success and happiness in life.

On a related note, I do not mind asking questions and do not mind admitting when I am not knowledgeable about something. I believe that you shouldn't be afraid to ask questions. In fact, I feel that admitting to your own weaknesses opens doors for you, and gives you the greatest capacity to learn even more than you already know.

I will never forget the time when I was Chair of the School Board and I had to read a document that had the word extemporaneously in it. Well first off, I'm not too proud to admit that I had to ask my friend Anne Meadows how to say it! And even then it still took me a few days just to be able to pronounce it! Ha!

But when I did, I did it well and the Superintendent smiled, knowing that it was not a word I would normally use myself!

The thing I always try to remember is that there is no one in this world who knows everything or can do everything. And by pretending to know something, you lose the chance to learn and grow. But by admitting your own weakness, you show those around you that you do not think that you are better than they are, but are simply another human being like they are.

And let's face it: we're all human!

Three: *Every day is a gift and it needs to be opened.*

There are two things I really mean here, although they are closely related. One is that you should look for pleasure and satisfaction from the mundane. The second is that you should let yourself go a little crazy sometimes and release your inner child. Both of these approaches to life are really states of mind. And they're about attitude.

Whether it's running my restaurant in Ogunquit, Maine (and the associated sweeping, cooking, cleaning and taking orders) or it's going on one of the many field trips I've taken with my children, I try to enjoy life to its fullest and not worry about whether what I'm doing will raise eyebrows from those who are less open-minded and carefree than I am. If they want to limit their own actions to "acceptable adult conduct" or to activities that they don't feel are "menial" then they are really missing out in my book.

For example, some people just go through the motions when they sweep the floor. They don't care about the results really, but just feel a sense of obligation to moving a broom back and forth across the floor. It's a boring task to them. There's no joy in the work because they aren't looking to the result of the sweeping—they're focusing on the fact that they've already had a long day, they're exhausted, and the last thing they want to do is to move their tired arms enough to clean a dirty floor that just can't stay clean for even an entire day.

When I'm sweeping, I'm looking at the floor and trying to find the bits that I've missed because I want the floor to be spotless. I'm thinking about the result (having a floor that is clean enough to make me proud) and I basically forget about the rest of it—the fact that I'm tired and that I'd rather be starting a new company or reading a book or playing with my kids. The act of sweeping the floor isn't boring to me—it's something that has to be done, so not only do I do it with a smile, but I figure I should do it well.

That's the side of *every day being a gift* where you look beyond the routine and the mundane and you remind yourself why even the simple things are important and have value. After all, as adults we all have responsibilities. But how we manage those responsibilities, or rather the attitude we exhibit while we are meeting those responsibilities, determines how happy we are as adults *most of the time.*

On the other side, I like to encourage people to remember the world as they saw it and lived in it when they were kids. Now I realize that you can't go around acting like a kid all day. You have responsibilities, after all. And there is a right time and a right place for being wild or crazy. And, depending upon your job, there might be a need to be more circumspect about things. But you also can't go around acting like a boring, responsible adult all the time because it's just a lot harder to feed your soul that way.

Apparently my soul needs a lot of feeding! Because I try to push the boundaries of acceptable behavior in whatever I do. I try to blur the lines of being responsible and having fun as often as I possibly can. Granted, I am fortunate enough to be more in control of that aspect of my life than many people because I run my own business. But the key point I'm making here is that I think most adults are not feeding their souls enough. They are not silly enough or crazy enough. And they don't ever let their hair down.

And that's a big part of why I love kids so much. I love kids. I really do. You can ask anyone in the Wells-Ogunquit School District why Sue Pollard is on the school board and they will tell you the same thing.

As a matter of fact, I was told just last week by one of the administrators that if I were to leave the school board that it would be a huge loss for the district. They felt that I was one of the few who truly were on the board for the right reasons. Those reasons are: my love for children, always being there for the underdog, and always trying to get funding for new ideas for the district. Above all, the biggest reason is that I'm active and engaged.

For me, if I can make a difference in a child's life, then it was worth sitting in all those boring school board meetings! Nothing personal, of course, but I am not your typical school board member. I love excitement and I love to have fun. I wear mini-skirts and I surf with the best of them. I am constantly trying to feed my ravenous soul!

And because of how I am, I find that the kids relate to me better than they can many adults. As a kid I can remember thinking that too many adults were boring and had lost their senses of humor. So clearly I can relate to kids, too!

One thing that I love, and that brings me closer to my own children, as well as the other children in the community, is that I'm always volunteering for every field trip possible—mostly just to have fun and bond with the kids.

Last June, a week before my daughter Miranda's graduation, I was whitewater rafting with my other daughter Lauren's whole eighth grade class. I had a blast! Rafting is a great way to get your adrenaline pumping. And rafting with my kids let them know that I'm just like them, that I enjoy the same fun, crazy things that they do. And it makes us so much closer every time I do anything like that with them.

On the trip we took there is a giant rope swing that hangs out over the river. The kids called it the "Holy Cow Swing". And you can bet that I was one of the first to swing on it! Am I crazy? Maybe a little bit. But I like to think I'm just enjoying life to the fullest.

Bottom line: I've always felt that if you're not having fun, you're doing something wrong. So lighten up, will ya?

Four: Treat people the way that you want to be treated yourself.

I believe in being nice, never being condescending, and treating people the way I want to be treated. I believe that always treating others with respect and courtesy are two of the most important and defining things a person can do.

I believe these things because they are the right things to do. And I also know how badly *I* feel when someone doesn't treat me with respect or is rude to me. It stinks, frankly. And I just don't understand it. It's really just so *unnecessary*!

I believe that you should strive to be a role model for everyone you encounter. You should go out of your way to be nice to *every single person you come in contact with.*

You should give to others, give to charities, give time, give of yourself. You should always demonstrate a positive attitude and it will come back to you a thousand-fold—and when you least expect it!

You should find time to work with young people, volunteer at school, church, and community organizations. Give your gift of positive motivation and enthusiasm to others. Don't ever hoard it. It wasn't given to you for that reason. I truly believe that every gift that was given to us was meant for us to share.

The Superintendent of our school, Ed McDonough, once told me that if there were any single person he knew who always had a positive attitude toward life, that it was me.

"No matter what the circumstance, you always look on the bright side. You have a way about you that when you walk into a room everyone smiles."

I always get great satisfaction from lifting people's confidence and encouraging others. If someone is having a bad day, I enjoy transforming their mood and lifting their spirits into a positive place—just as I appreciate others doing the same for me. I don't think there is anything I enjoy more than seeing someone respect and encourage someone else. All of these things feed me, and give me more energy. And while I don't do all of this because I expect anything in return, I also believe strongly that the good that you do will come back to you.

I remember talking to my neighbor Tom Bannister at one point during the Survivor process. He was so supportive of me when I confided with him that I had applied to be on Survivor. He was always encouraging, and always positive. He would tell me that they'd have to be crazy not to take me, and that he knew I was going to make it. Tom knows me well, and he knew, despite my confidence, that I was anxious about whether I would make it. So he was there for me. That's what doing good does for you. It brings you closer to people.

Every positive action you take to help someone in need weaves a net of support and encouragement for you (and for them—since it really is infectious!). The more threads in your net, the larger and stronger it becomes. The stronger your net is, the more likely it is to help you. And when the net gets large enough it can encompass an entire community.

At the extremes, a strong net could help you catch more, and bigger, fish. Or, looking at it another way, a strong net could help to catch *you* when you might otherwise have fallen to the rocks at the bottom of a proverbial cliff.

I would say that this is probably my most important principle (of the first six, anyway—since number seven incorporates this one within it).

Treat people the way you want to be treated, and all of the rest will just happen.

Five: Don't rely on others for your happiness or you'll too often be disappointed.

I start every day with a big smile and a great attitude because I don't know one person who doesn't like being around a positive person. On the other side of the coin, I don't know a single person who *does like* to be around a negative person. How basic is that concept? I mean, come on!

Think about it: Is there really a choice? I can hear the internal "debate" now.

I think I will hang around Gertrude today (no offense to any Gertrude's in the audience!). *She's depressing. She doesn't have much going on with her life and when she goes home from work she doesn't do anything about her boredom and her loneliness but just plunks down in front of the television. She hates animals and always complains about her weight.*

Or . . .

I could hang around with Sue who is upbeat and dynamic, who loves life, and always has something good to say. She always makes me laugh and she's so active in the community: she volunteers for the children's reading groups and is Chair of the School Board. To top it all off, she thinks that anything is possible, if you believe!

Gee, that's probably going to be a hard decision!

I believe that happiness in life, and the enthusiasm to live it, comes from maintaining a positive attitude and that we all have the potential to be happy within us. If we're not careful, however, we also have the potential to spiral downward into negativity.

The key thing to recognize (and it's so obvious I really can't understand how it escapes so many people) is that exhibiting a positive attitude yourself actually creates and draws out even more positive energy from those around you. By the same token, exhibiting negativity only encourages a negative response from those around you.

We all enjoy being around positive people. It's just a basic survival instinct to avoid people who are too negative. Negative people are usually people who are very unhappy with their own life. And because I recognize this, whenever I encounter such a person I challenge myself and try my best to infect them with my condition: chronic enthusiasm!

Six: *Always keep family a priority.*

When I was young, and in junior high in particular, I struggled in my class-work and I loved sports—probably because it was an escape and a release for me. And because I loved it so much, I usually did very well with anything athletic.

My parents almost never came to my games because they always had to work. With five kids and all, it was tough for them. But it was tough for me too, because they never had the time to come and see me make the winning goal in field hockey, or win that important tennis match, or become the top ten swimmer in the state, or see me become the only kid in my junior year to receive my WSI (Water Safety Instructor) certification on award night.

It hurt not to be recognized by my parents for my accomplishments. It hurt not to be supported, whether I was successful or not, in something I loved to do. As a consequence I built a very tough wall around myself. I didn't want to continually get hurt and I wanted to hide my pain and my sadness at not having my parents there.

All of my other friends seemed to have their parents there cheering them on. And I had to learn, early on, to build up my wall and to become very tough on the outside. Of course, by doing so, no one ever knew how much I hurt on the inside.

And while some of the side effects of that wall were beneficial in their way (like my inner strength and self-reliance)—and are still with me today, and make me who I am in fact—not all of the side effects are positive.

I loved my dad and I love my mom very much. My father was a good person, very hard-working, honest, and well-intentioned. And my mother is the same way. They both gave me a great sense of humor and a true love for life. And I share many of the same values that they held so highly and imparted to me growing up.

And I like to think that if they could have been there for me, to support me in all of my activities, that they would have. I guess I've always believed that. But I still missed them when I was on the playing field. And I still built up my wall.

I'm sure in their minds they were providing us with everything we could possibly need. They were putting clothes on our backs and food on the table and keeping us warm and dry in a comfortable home. I can't fault them for their priorities. But I know how my childhood sometimes made me feel. And I want better for my own children. That's why, when I say that I put my family first, I mean something different from what my parents probably would have said.

For me, raising a child is a nurturing act. It is not enough simply to provide food, clothes and shelter for your children—or even guidance. All of these things can be seen, legitimately, as expressions of love and affection. The coalminer or fisherman who toils away for days at a time in hazardous conditions does so out of a selfless desire to provide for his family. And he can easily be justified in arguing that his sacrifices are the only demonstration he needs to give of his love for his family. But for me that just doesn't cut it.

Because I know how it felt to be emotionally neglected. And that neglect came at the worst possible time in my life—when I was going through all of the painful changes and challenges of youth, when I was trying to figure out who I was, when I hadn't quite figured out yet such important lessons as the fact that my own worth wasn't determined by who approved of me at my school.

And since doing well at sports made me popular with my peers I put as much energy into it as I could. And because I was intimidated by my teachers, I withered academically. In fact, I never did overcome that fear of teachers when I was in school. I carried it with me right up until my oldest child was getting old enough to go to school herself. Then it occurred to me that I needed to do something about my own fears, if I were going to be a model for my children. So what did I do to overcome my intimidation? I like to think that I confronted the situation in my own classic style: I ran for and became elected as Chair of the School Board!

So, what do I mean when I say that I believe family should be a priority? Well, I mean that you should try to teach your children everything you know. You should motivate them. Whenever possible you should treat them as equals. You should be positive. Encourage them to take action and be independent. And, to me, this last one is especially important: you should always *be there* for your children.

They need to know that you are there for them whenever you can be, even when you're not physically at their side. I was prepared (and still am!) to leave my family for 40 days in order to be a contestant on Survivor. Yet I know in my heart, as much as I would miss them and they would miss me, that they would know that I was there for them. Even on the most remote island in the world my children would know that I love them and they would know that I was going to come home and be there for them once again.

I've done everything I can to nurture my children in the hopes that they never feel neglected, and they never feel that they can't come to me with any problem they might have. I am their friend. And they are my friends, too.

Seven: Always "Rock on!"

So what is "Rock on!", anyway? For me, it's really a combination of the other six principles. And it's also about taking all seven of them on the road and touching the lives of people around me. "Rock on!" means doing good deeds, making stuff happen, and preaching my own personal gospel of maintaining a positive attitude in all aspects of my life. When I tell someone to "Rock on!" what I'm telling them is to go out and kick some ass and take some names. To be active and not passive. To be motivated and motivating. And to make a difference out in the world by being a role model for kindness and generosity and compassion and *action*!

I'll give you an example . . .

I went into school one day to give three people the winnings from a diet competition that I had put on right after Christmas. What inspired me to start this diet challenge? Well, I was starting in on a new exercise routine myself and I wanted to share my energy and my desire to help people feel better about themselves.

The Alternate Survivor

I started the weight loss challenge on January 9, 2006 (to help people shed their holiday weight!). I was hoping to get a fair number of competitors and, to my surprise, I got an overwhelming response. There were fifty people who joined this little diet challenge which ran until April 3, 2006.

Everyone who joined needed to be committed. So I asked each of them to put in one hundred dollars. The three people who lost the highest percentage of their body weight would each win a cash prize.

For the first six weeks I weighed everyone in and e-mailed the results to the whole group. The idea was to make people work harder by showing the progress of their competition. All in good fun! Then on the last six-weeks you were on your own—so there was an element of the unknown that came into the competition. Would people work harder out of fear that their competition was losing weight faster than they were?

When sending out the e-mails every week I would also put in positive quotes like the following to try to help motivate people:

Those who Push the Hardest ~
See the Greatest Results! "Rock On"

The only people who never fail ~
Are those who never try! "Rock On"

YES YOU CAN! There is no such thing as "Can't". See your goals in your mind's eye. Know that you can achieve them. Work tirelessly; sweating, developing and utilizing resources you never knew you had . . . and success will be yours!

The responses I got were often just as much fun. I was getting energy back from the group as much as I was giving it! It really was a blast and was a very encouraging competition for everyone involved.

Now you're probably wondering, *Sue, why would you do all of this work and all of this running around and not make any money out of it?* I guess you'd just have to know me! I love making a difference and motivating people and the bottom line is that it's not always (and shouldn't be) just about making money. When you're well-liked, trusted and always in a happy mood, success in life will just happen for you.

So back to my story . . . The day of the final weigh-in was here: April 3, 2006! And may I say that I could not have been more proud of so many people that worked so unbelievably hard! In just twelve short weeks we had lost 940 pounds as a group! Awesome!

I sent out specific times for people to weigh in and they all started showing up. Everyone had smiles on their faces. Most were wearing smaller clothes. I must have said about 50 times "Oh, my gosh! You look awesome! I'm so proud of you!" Again and again and again I spoke the same words. What a tremendous effort from everyone in the group!

The only hard part was that there could only be three winners. I went home and I did all the calculations. Then I had my husband double-check my math. Finally, when I was satisfied that I'd gotten it right, I e-mailed everyone the results that night at around 10:30.

The next day I went out to give the top three winners their prize money. Dan, who won first place, is the Athletic Director and Physical Education teacher at the junior high. And I was bringing him his prize last.

I walked in with my twelve-year-old son Justin, who Dan coaches, and I had Justin hand him the thirty-five hundred dollars in brand-new, one hundred dollar bills. Justin said, "Mr. MacLeod? I heard that out of all the teachers you were the Biggest Loser!" (I can't imagine where my kid *gets* it, can you?!)

Then, with a big smile, Justin gave his coach a high five, said congratulations, and handed him the money.

After I praised Dan and said what a great job he had done, he took out one of his new hundred dollar bills and said, "Sue, this is for you. I would have never done this, or won this, if you hadn't put the whole thing together."

I said, "No that's all for you, Dan. You worked hard, so why don't you buy something at Disney for your kids!" I knew he was going to use the money he had won to take his four children and wife to Disney.

He just smiled and said to my son "Justin, you know if there were more people in the world like your mom, this world would be a much better place." Justin smiled and said, "I know!"

God love both of them!

On the same day, when I was walking into Dan's office, he had been lecturing a young boy about not doing well on a test because he didn't believe the boy had been trying his best. There was certainly nothing wrong with what Dan was doing. He was a teacher trying to discipline a seventh grader who he didn't believe was giving his best effort.

But when I overheard what the conversation was about, I remembered a little girl (me!) who had similar problems when she was young. She didn't try. Then, when she fell behind, she tried even less. In fact, she spiraled downward academically and never really pulled herself out of it. I remember that, for me, speeches and lectures by my teachers and parents didn't work. Once I'd done poorly on a test, it was already too late. What I had really needed was for people to talk to me and encourage me beforehand. I had needed the attention and the support all along, in fact. And yelling at me or trying to make me feel bad when the damage was already done just never, ever worked.

Of course, I wasn't thinking that it was too late for this seventh grader! But I do believe that poor performance on a test from an otherwise intelligent child is a good sign that something needs to change in the boy's life or his education to get him back on track. Maybe this was an isolated incident. Maybe the boy would learn from his own mistakes and turn himself around. But maybe it was a sign that for this particular child he needed something that he wasn't getting.

I could have waited quietly outside Dan's office door for them to finish and then gone in to talk with Dan when the boy had left. But I don't believe in sitting idly by while I witness something that I think I can push in the right direction. Plus, I have a soft spot for kids—and especially for the underdog!

So when the 7th grader was leaving I asked if I could talk to him for a minute. The young boy was just about in tears. He was trying to keep his poise and keep his chin up.

I said, "Can I talk to you for a minute?"

"Yup." He nodded his head.

We walked out of Dan's office and went out and sat in the hall.

I said, "Nothing seems easy does it?"

He shook his head, *no.*

I said, "Believe it or not, that's a good thing. I can tell just by looking at you, that you're someone who really cares and you're mad you didn't do well on that test. Aren't you?"

Again he nodded.

Then I said, "ADMIT IT!" with a big smile.

He smiled back somewhat sheepishly and said, "I could have done better."

I said, "There you go! We all have off days. I remember taking tests in school and not getting very good grades. Why? Because I didn't study for them and I wasn't prepared. So whose fault was that? MINE!" I said.

He laughed, and I continued, "The point I'm trying to make is that we all try to sneak by once in a while and not get caught. But when it comes to preparing or not preparing for a test, the bottom line is that we're only really letting ourselves down if we don't give it our best effort.

"I've seen you in sports. You're good. So don't short yourself. You're worth more than that."

I put up my hand for a high five. He didn't leave me hanging (Thank God!) and slapped me five.

"Now go have a great day, because you're worth every minute of it!"

He smiled and started to walk off and then turned and said "Mrs. Pollard? You have a good day, too."

I winked at him and, being the sap that I am, I teared up and felt awesome! I felt like I'd just had my own little Mean Joe Green moment!

My day went on to be awesome! I talked to so many more people who had been on the diet challenge and each one stopped me in the hall to tell me how motivating the competition had been.

"Sue, I just want to thank you for doing all the work in putting this challenge together!"

"I feel great!"

"I am exercising for the first time in I don't know how long!"

"I feel like a new person!"

The Alternate Survivor

I was hugging everybody and complimenting them on what a great job they all had done. There are no words that can express the feeling you get when you make a difference in someone's life. I feel truly gifted to be able to help and motivate people in a positive way.

I feel so blessed. Trust me, if you were to try doing something like this yourself, then you would feel the same way. But what if doing something like this takes you out of your comfort zone? Well, I can tell you that once you've done it a single time you'll be hooked for life! I don't even remember a time when going out of my way to help others was difficult, frankly. And the more I've done things like this, the more second-nature it has become.

For me the bottom line is that if I can make someone's day a happier one, then I have accomplished everything that matters! Isn't that what life is truly about?

"Rock On"!

Eight

An Open Letter to Mark Burnett

Dear Mark,

I tried everything to get your attention. I wrote you over
100 letters. I made you personalized postcards. I sent
you more motivational words than you'd hear if you spent
a month with Tony Robbins. I could have quit and just let
it go like Dana suggested. But, like I told you in person:
quitting isn't an option for me. You left me with no other
choice as I saw it but to write this book.

So what do I want? Really? I'm truly not kidding you when I tell you that all I want is another chance to be on Survivor. I hope you can respect what I'm trying to do here. I hope you appreciate that all of this is because I was captivated by your creation.

You're an inspiring man. I bought and read all of your books. And in those books I read all about your entrepreneurial spirit, your goals, and your motivation—about jumping in and taking chances.

Well, that's just what I'm doing, Mark.

But I'm not coming empty-handed, because I have a proposition for you. I'd like to challenge you to your own game. Literally.

You and me: as *contestants* on *Survivor*.

Crazy? Nahhh. I know that you used to do this stuff—back in the Eco-Challenge days. And before that you were a paratrooper. And I know that you really enjoyed it, too! For that matter, I've heard Jeff Probst say on more than one occasion how he'd love the opportunity to play himself.

Don't tell me that the idea isn't appealing. Your show is awesome—one of the best shows in the history of television and certainly the best thing on the air right now. But wouldn't a little extra spice and a bit of a change-up be nice about now?

So what do you say? Why don't we play? I have some great ideas on how the competition might work, too!

My favorite idea is that you could call up all of the *Survivor* Contestants who missed the cut by one. And I could be their Captain. We would be the *Alternate Survivors,* of course. And for your team you might select a group of Survivor All-Stars. Or maybe you'd prefer the company of a group of *celebrity* Survivors. As long as I'm there, I'm happy to be flexible. It *is* your show, after all!

I have more ideas, but I'll save my thoughts about how the actual competition itself might work for our phone call. After all, a girl has to have *some* secrets!

Oh and by the way, I'm not giving this a rest or quitting until you say yes. That's why I wrote the book.

I'm ready to take it on Oprah. I'm ready to take it on Good Morning America. I'll take it anywhere I can until you take me seriously and give me a chance.

One way or the other, I *will* play *Survivor*!

Looking forward to your call, Mark!

Sincerely,

Sue Pollard

The Alternate Survivor

Nine

Closing Remarks

I feel like I got my own foot in the door with *Survivor* and the *Amazing Race*. But there have been times that I've wondered, looking back, if maybe Lynne Spillman and the rest of the *Survivor* casting crew might not have felt bad for what they had put me through, and especially how they had just left me hanging. And I've considered the possibility that maybe my shot at *Big Brother* was a way for them to give me an opportunity for something else.

But then I woke up. And I remembered that I am just a commodity to them—and either useful to them or not, at their whim and discretion. And even if they felt bad at all for how I'd been jerked around like a puppet during the *Survivor* casting process, they still wouldn't have put me up for *Big Brother* if they didn't see something in me that might work on the show.

On the one hand, I felt good that people were seeing something in me that they thought the American people would be interested in getting to know. But on the other hand, the sense that they believed people were just tools at their disposal had crept into my mind and I couldn't shake it.

Looking back on the whole thing now I think about Mark Burnett's vision and the core concept behind all of his shows, and I question whether he might have strayed from his original intentions. Essentially, he insists that the most important dramatic elements of his shows revolve around the regular people who are on them: their natural and personal responses to the challenges before them, their individual interactions with each other, and the "realness" of their often emotional triumphs or failures. And it makes me think a couple different things:

First off, it makes me think that Mark Burnett wouldn't be proud of how I was treated. I feel as though, if I were to tell him my side of the story, he would recognize the disconnect between his vision of what *Survivor* is really all *about* and how the selection process is operated.

I am not an actor. And that's exactly what Mark Burnett claims to want on his shows: *non-actors*. But by the same token I am not accustomed to being treated like livestock the way that professional actors might be, who are more familiar with casting calls. And so there you have the great irony of the whole thing: they wanted people to be as desperate for the "part" on the show as an out-of-work actor (doing whatever they were told, patiently accepting the long waits and the odd and tyrannical rules, etc.) but then, come show time, they wanted "real" responses and nothing of the human element of the show to be staged or acted out.

On the other hand, I think that maybe Mark Burnett would listen to my story and when he came to understand what I was saying, rather than empathizing or apologizing, he might decide that he wanted to do a show on the casting process itself because he wouldn't be able to help but see the potential of the human interest angle in the experience. And speaking from personal experience, I can tell you that while the smile never left *my* face during those eleven days in California *(and beyond)* I had gone through a *whole range* of emotions!

As I discovered when I ultimately realized that I wouldn't be participating on *Survivor 6: Amazon*, you need to learn how to make your own way in whatever situation you face and to create your own success. I could have just accepted that I didn't make it. It was disappointing for sure. I had tried to show them that I would make the perfect *Survivor*. I had been myself and I had believed that the things that were important to me, and that I stood for, would be the things that would convince the casting team to select me for the show.

But it didn't work out that way. It stinks. And I wish they could have known me better so they would have realized how much fun and energy and enthusiasm I would have added to the show. But I'm not giving up, either. I wrote this book to tell my story. And I wrote it because so many of my friends have asked me what the whole experience was like and I realized that there isn't a book already out there that tells about the *Survivor* casting experience. But I also wrote it because I wanted to rise above this whole experience and make something good come of what was really a difficult personal defeat for me.

And the last reason I wrote the book is that I wanted to get Mark Burnett's attention—and give him another chance. Ha! But seriously, Mark, if you're out there reading this or if someone who knows Mark is reading this, have him give me a call. And I'll be ready to go at a moment's notice—just like I was back in 2002.

Oh yeah, I almost forgot: 'Rock on!"

Acknowledgements

I've tried to remember everyone who has been there for me throughout this process (some from the very beginning, and some only having joined me recently), but please forgive me if I haven't mentioned you below. And in case I have forgotten anyone, I'd like to say thank you to the entire Ogunquit community. I truly feel like we are all one extended family!

Okay, here goes:

To start, I need to thank my Lord and Savior Jesus Christ for giving me so many gifts, including perseverance, tenacity, the gift of making people laugh, and the gift of encouraging others. Every single one of us has been given a special gift from Him and so many choose not to use them. How sad! I would like to tell each one of you, if you ever wondered if Christ really does exist, that the answer is yes! This book would never have happened if Jesus Christ did not give me the innovation and vision to prevail! Jesus opened doors I didn't even know existed. Things happened and people came into my life only through the work of Jesus Christ.

I was driving in my car six months ago, delivering an order to LL Bean. On the way home from Freeport, I asked Jesus, "Am I supposed to be doing this book?" The next second I looked at a license plate and it read "SURVIVR!" Call it coincidental, if you will, but for all of you Christians out there you know that was a sign from God!

Then, to top it off just last week, I was driving around in Ogunquit and I was talking to God as I often do and I prayed. I prayed that May 27th, my first book signing, would be a sunny day. I looked at

the car coming at me and the license plate read
"Faith"—as if to say *I've got you covered*! Again,
coincidental? I don't think so! Jesus, thank you for
being by my side and never letting me go!

I would also like to thank Bethany Church at
Breakfast Hill in Greenland N.H. and Pastor Bruce
Boria. People often ask me why we drive all the way
from Ogunquit to Greenland just to go to church. I
only have one thing to say: You'd have to come to
Bethany yourself to experience it!

To Pastor Bruce Boria: "Yo Babe, Rock On!"

Next, I need to thank my great family: my
husband Bob and my three awesome kids Miranda,
Lauren and Justin. Don't worry guys, when I finally
make it, were going to Hawaii and we're really gonna
surf!

My writer and my new best friend: Matt Berg,
who was introduced to me by Randy Cushman. I
told Randy I was seriously thinking about writing a
book about everything that happened. I went into
the details with him and his first response was, '*Do I
have the perfect guy for you! Not only is he an*

unbelievable writer but he's determined, competitive and talk about not taking no for an answer: Matt doesn't even understand that word!' I was introduced to Matt last August and he has now become my anchor, my rock. There is no one I would have been more pleased to work with than Matt Berg! Thank you so much, Randy Cushman—I love you!

Then there is the man who started me on this whole process: Richard Payeur. Don't worry, Richard, I have something special in store for you! Thank you so much, Richard. There are no words to say except *thank you for believing in me.*

Thank you Peggy and Sharma Damren! Boy, do we go back in time! You are, and always will be, the greatest and the last of the Mohicans. I love you both very much!

Bobby Winn: one of my favorite motivators! Don't quit yet, Babe! We'll make it on Amazing Race one way or the other! Love ya!

The Alternate Survivor

Jeff Rodman, Ed McDonough, and Ira Waltz—three people who love kids just as much as I do! We're so lucky to have people like you supporting our children and teaching them values that will be a part of their lives forever! To all three of you I have only one thing to say, "ROCK ON!"

Anne Meadows. What can I say? You're awesome! You have been an advocate for me since day one. For those of you who don't know Anne, she is the Superintendent of Schools' secretary and there's nothing this woman can't do. Even extemporaneously! Ha! I love you, Anne!

Karen Audet, a dear friend of mine for many years who always lends an ear when I most need it. Karen and I have had many laughs over this process. I also want to thank you, Karen, for believing in me! Love ya!

Thank you, Judy Yates! Judy has worked for the town for twenty five plus years. She's a great friend of mine and has been with me since this process started. She is an inspiration and most of all a very true friend. You're the best, Judy!

Tom Bannister. If you ever need to tell someone something and you don't want anyone to find out about it, Tom's your man. I confided in him at various points in this process knowing that he was a Survivor buff and he never even told his wife Joan! Tom, you're the best! Thank you for always being so positive. I guess you were right: one way or another I will make it on Survivor!

Last but not least, my Mom. There are no words! (As my eyes fill up with tears!) I love you so much! You have taught me to be the invincible woman that I am today. You've taught me courage, tenacity and most of all you've taught me how to love. I want you to know that I understand now about how you and Dad weren't able to be there for my sports. Believe it or not you taught me the greatest lesson of all: As long as I knew you were in my heart, you and dad were right there on those fields with me! Thank you for being the greatest

Mom in the world! I know Dad is smiling down from heaven saying, *'That's my girl!'*

To all of you out there reading this book who believe in me: I *am* going to make it!

Sue

05/07/2006